THE
SHINING
PRINCESS

AND OTHER
JAPANESE LEGENDS

ERIC QUAYLE
Illustrated by MICHAEL FOREMAN

Arcade Publishing · New York

Little, Brown and Company

Text Copyright © 1989 by Eric Quayle
Illustrations Copyright © 1989 by Michael Foreman
All rights reserved. No part of this book may be
reproduced in any form or by any electronic or
mechanical means, including information storage and
retrieval systems, without permission in writing from
the publisher, except by a reviewer who may quote
brief passages in a review.

First U.S. Edition
First published in Great Britain by Andersen Press Limited
Library of Congress Cataloguing-in-Publication Data is available
Library of Congress Catalog Card Number 89-84076

ISBN 1-55970-039-4

Published in the United States by Arcade Publishing, Inc.,
New York, a Little, Brown company
Printed in Italy
1 3 5 7 9 10 8 6 4 2

Contents

For my Japanese-speaking twin daughters,
Aprilla and Dabriella

Introduction

The earliest translations of traditional Japanese fairy tales into English were made in 1888. A series of twenty little booklets, printed on soft-textured paper from coloured wood-blocks, were exported to Britain, there to be issued by Griffith Farran & Co., London, in specially made drop-fronted boxes.

The three original translators were the great Japanologist Basil Hall Chamberlain, Emeritus Professor of Japanese in Tokyo University; the Reverend David Thompson, an American missionary in Japan; and Mrs T.H. James, a resident in the British colony in Yokohama, who had delighted her children and their friends by reading her versions to them.

It was not until fifteen years later that the Japanese themselves attempted a translation of their fairy legends into English. *The Japanese Fairy Book*, 1903, was compiled by Yei Theodora Ozaki, and contained twenty-two tales with illustrations by the Tokyo artist Kakuzo Fujiyama.

These were the sources I used in compiling the present work, embellished by the oral tradition of listening to my Japanese wife Sachiko telling bedtime stories to my three bi-lingual children, Eden, aged nine, and our eight-year-old twin girls Aprilla and Dabriella. As an added treat they will now have my friend and colleague Michael Foreman's restlessly creative illustrations to wonder about.

Zennor,
Cornwall

ERIC QUAYLE

The Shining Princess

Long, long ago, there lived an old bamboo woodcutter called Genzo and his wife. Not only were they very poor but they were often very sad for heaven had not seen fit to send them a child and both of them dearly loved little children.

The old man knew that there could be no rest from work, for he and his wife had only just enough to eat with the little money he made by selling his cut bamboo, no rest that is until he was laid in a quiet grave amongst the groves of bamboo with his wife beside him.

On this particular morning he had gone out to work as usual armed with his axe, its edge razor sharp, and had started on an unusually green clump of bamboo. In Japan bamboo often grows over ten metres high and this was a particularly tall and healthy group. He had felled only a couple of stems when the grove was suddenly diffused with a silvery glow, more like moonlight than the rays of the sun. Genzo looked round in astonishment and then realised that the light was pouring from the very first shoot he had cut. The old man dropped his axe and peeped into the severed stump and there, to his amazement, sitting contentedly in the hollow stem, was the prettiest little girl he had ever seen. Girl, he called her, but she was actually a

miniature human being, only a few centimetres high but perfect in every respect.

She smiled up at Genzo, light radiating from her as he stooped to lift the little creature.

'The gods must have sent you to be our child for it was in the bamboo that I, a poor bamboo cutter, found you.' And Genzo bowed low to show his thanks.

His wife could hardly believe her eyes when her husband hurried home before midday, but her astonishment was even greater when he opened his cupped hands and revealed the tiny little child.

'Can we keep her? Can we keep her? Please say we can!'

They were now an extremely happy old couple and were made even more so when Genzo-san began to find little lumps of pure gold every now and then. These were always inside the hollow stems of the bamboo he cut down, not in every one by any means but about once a week he would see the gleam of gold and excitedly fish out yet another nugget. Occasionally he would find a precious stone in the same hiding places, a diamond, a ruby, a sapphire, and even a flawless pearl or two.

By degrees the happy old couple became quite rich so that they were able to move to a larger and finer house. It was here that they named their child Kaguyahime, a Japanese name translated as 'The Shining Princess'. She was a princess who was growing rapidly, astonishingly so, for in only three months she had progressed from a tiny doll-like creature into a fully-grown young lady of surpassing beauty. In a darkened room she glowed with a soft radiance so that the old couple addressed her as Princess Moonlight. All those lucky enough to be allowed to see her were dazzled by her loveliness and could hardly wait to spread the tale of what they had seen.

Before long her fame was known in far off Kyoto and even in the outer islands of Japan, and suitors for her hand in marriage came knocking and bowing and pleading for a chance to see the Shining Princess. All were refused permission except for three knights whom Princess Moonlight had secretly selected from the crowd of suitors who jostled for places in the garden beneath her window. With all the

rest dismissed each of the three was allowed to enter the lower room
for a brief glimpse of their bride-to-be, only to be left speechless at her
glowing radiance.

'If you are to win my hand,' she told each of them in turn, 'you must
complete the task I set you.'

She asked the first knight to bring her back a branch of the
wonderful tree which grew on the summit of Mount Horai in the far
distant Eastern Sea. The roots of this tree were of silver, the trunk of
gold, and its branches bore diamonds in the shape of flowers. The
knight bowed low and withdrew, still unable to speak a word.

The second knight she asked to bring her back from China the skin
of the fire-rat. This extremely rare, but ferocious animal always
attacked on sight and its bite was lethal. It also had the magical power
of being completely immune to flames and heat and could walk
through the hottest fire without harm. The second knight bowed low
and withdrew in silence.

Princess Moonlight asked the third knight to search for the dragon
that carried a precious stone embedded in the centre of its scaly head,
a stone that shone with five separate colours and which could make

17

you invisible by merely stroking it. So the third knight made his bow and withdrew.

Each of the three went their separate ways and, having seen her beauty for themselves, each was determined to win the hand of the Shining Princess.

However, all three knew that the tasks they had been set were quite beyond their powers so each in turn set about devising a scheme that would trick the Princess into thinking they had succeeded.

The first knight did indeed set out for Mount Horai, but having heard that its slopes were the haunt of giant serpents and that the tree itself was guarded by fire-breathing dragons he turned aside to the town of Yamaguchi. It was a city famous for its silversmiths and the first knight sought out the very best and promised them much gold if they could copy exactly a branch of the wonderful tree which grew on the summit of Mount Horai. The jewellers set to work and for a whole year they used their skills until they finished the golden branch with its diamonds in the shape of flowers. The knight paid them well and set off back to the home of the Shining Princess with his gift carefully protected in a silk-lined box of the finest split bamboo.

Meanwhile, the second knight had sailed for China in quest of the vicious fire-rat, only to be told that the last six warriors who had attempted to catch it had each been bitten to death and their bodies consumed in flames. Why should he take such a risk, he asked himself, when a cunning Chinese magician could make a skin so like that of the fire-rat that no one in the world could tell the difference?

He searched for many months before finding a magician willing to undertake the task and much gold changed hands before the skin was finally produced. Well satisfied, the second knight set off back to Japan with his precious gift laid in a lacquered box adorned with silver and precious stones.

The third knight had set off in search of the dragon which carried a fabulous ruby embedded in the centre of its scaly head, but as he approached the cave in which it lived he came upon stacks of blackened skulls and other human bones. As he paused in fear there came a roar from the cave and a puff of smoke and flame so that he

instantly turned his horse's head and galloped at full speed away across the plains. Even so he felt a whiff of heat at his back, but this caused his horse to gallop even faster and thus saved his life.

Like the the first two knights, he now sought out a skilful jeweller and set him the task of exactly imitating the precious stone set in the dragon's head, a type of ruby which shone with five separate colours and had magical powers. In a year the stone was delivered to him at the cost of much gold, and the third knight, too, set off for the home of the Shining Princess.

When the first knight arrived at the home of the Shining Princess he immediately asked old Genzo and his wife to take the bamboo box and its precious contents to their lovely daughter now that he had completed his task successfully. The old couple hurried to the Princess and laid the box at her feet, retiring to kneel at the edge of the room while she undid the silken ribbons. When she took out the golden branch with its glittering flowers they gasped with wonder, only to fall silent as they saw her frown.

'A bough from the tree on Mount Horai is warm and gentle to the touch, magically warm from the fires in the mountain's heart. But this imitation I hold in my hand is cold and metallic. Take the false thing away!' And the Shining Princess fluttered her fan in anger.

When Genzo handed back the golden bough to the knight and told him he was dismissed the warrior stamped his foot in rage and crashed the precious object to the floor. He turned his horse's head towards the mountains and was never seen in Genzo's province again. The Princess gave orders that the gold and jewels were to be sold and the money given to the poor people of the district. They ever afterwards blessed her name.

Next day the second knight arrived and handed over the lacquer box containing the skin of the fire-rat. The Princess opened the box, undid the silken wrappings and took out the skin and examined it carefully.

'It looks and feels just like the skin of a fire-rat, but there is one sure test I must make.'

She carried the skin over to the glowing brazier and dropped it on the hottest part of the fire. Within seconds the skin shrivelled and emitted an acrid black smoke, then suddenly burst into flames.

'Again a false object has been brought to me. Even the fiercest flame could not singe a single hair of a fire-rat. Send that dishonest knight away!' And once again the Shining Princess fluttered her fan in anger.

When the warrior was told the news he turned his horse's head towards the mountains and galloped away and that was the end of him.

The third knight arrived a day later and handed over the enamel box containing the jewel, telling Genzo that he had personally slain the dragon and then prised the ruby from its bony head. The old man hurried away and handed the Princess the box. At first she seemed quite impressed with the precious stone, turning it in her hand so that it changed into five beautiful colours each catching the light with glowing rays.

'Perhaps this third knight is a true knight,' said the Princess, 'but I must give the stone its final test.' She started to stroke the ruby, then turned to the old couple and asked them if they could still see her.

'Of course we can, Princess Moonlight!'

'Then once again they have tried to trick me. The real dragon stone would have made me invisible. Take the miserable thing away!'

So with the third knight banished from her sight Princess Moonlight now had no suitors for her hand and she told the old couple that this pleased her rather than made her sad.

'I will always remain a single girl so I can live with you until my time here on earth is up.'

Genzo and his wife were overjoyed, although a little puzzled by what she meant by her 'time here on earth' being finished.

So they all lived happily for many years until the time came when the Shining Princess took to sitting for hours every night on the balcony gazing up at the moon. She appeared to be growing sadder and sadder, until one night the old man found her weeping as though her heart would break. He pleaded with her to tell what it was that was making her so upset, until finally, with many tears, she told him that her time on earth would soon be finished and the reason why she was so sad was that she could not bear to leave Genzo and his wife, her foster-parents, but that she must return to her real parents and her former home on the moon.

'It is ordained that on the fifteenth of this month of August the Moon People will come to take me back. I cannot refuse, but I promise to return to you as often as I can. Look for me at every full moon.'

It was just as she said. When, on the fifteenth of August, the yellow harvest moon rose high in the heavens Princess Moonlight bade the old couple goodbye and, as they closed their eyes to pray for her safe return she faded from sight and was gone.

Genzo and his wife lived good and healthy lives to a very old age, happy at knowing that they saw the Shining Princess every single month, for when the full moon rose in the heavens her room would glow with light and they would hear her voice calling to them. Until daylight they would talk happily with her, accepting the gift she always brought and giving her their love in return.

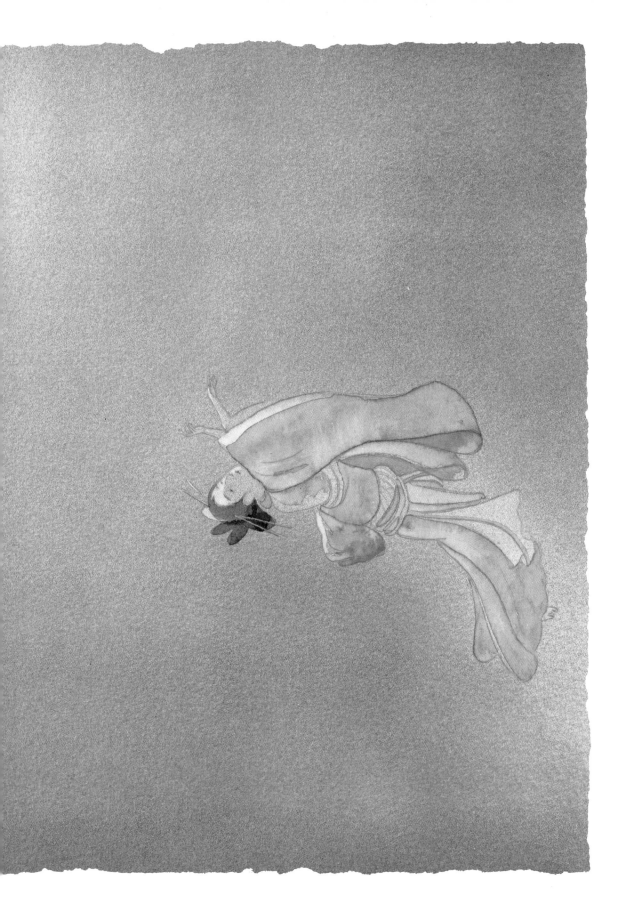

The White Hare and the Crocodiles

There was a time, long long ago, when all the animals in Japan could talk, and even the birds and the fishes could understand what Man was saying.

Now it so happened that on the island of Oki, just across the sea from the mainland of Inaba, there lived a little white hare. He had explored his island countless times and his one wish was to visit the mainland and see the rest of the world. But how to cross the sea, that was the trouble? Day after day, as soon as he had finished breakfast, he would go down to the shore to gaze longingly to the distant outline of Inaba, and day after day he would puzzle to find a way to cross the water.

Then the unexpected happened! He was sitting as usual with his paws on the sand when he saw, swimming towards him, a large and aggressive-looking crocodile.

'What a piece of luck,' said the hare to himself. 'I'll ask my scaly friend to let me ride on his back right across the sea to Inaba.'

But at that moment the crocodile saw the little white hare and opened its mouth to smile a greeting. It was the sight of the rows of sharp white teeth that made our friend the hare hesitate. If the crocodile started to feel hungry when they were halfway across, for instance . . .! There must be other ways, less dangerous. He put his paw to his head and thought.

Then in his most friendly voice he called across the water: 'Isn't it a lovely day, Mr Crocodile?'

The crocodile had been feeling lonely for some hours and being a very talkative creature he immediately welcomed the opportunity to pass the time of day with the furry little animal sitting there on the sand dunes.

'It is a lovely day, Mr Rabbit.'

'Hare, actually.'

'Pardon?'

'I'm a hare. We are bigger and far more intelligent than rabbits, and of course we can run three or four times as fast. But tell me, Mr Crocodile, something I've always wanted to know. You live in the sea and I live on land, but do you think there are as many crocodiles as there are hares?'

'Of course there are more crocodiles than hares,' answered the reptile, swishing his scaly tail in amusement. 'Countless more!'

'Are you really sure?'

'I don't make statements I can't prove, Mr Hare.'

'But surely there could not possibly be enough crocodiles to stretch in a line all the way from this little island across the sea to distant Inaba? Not all the way to the mainland, surely?' And the hare smiled, then shook with laughter. 'You can't expect me to believe that. Not without actually seeing such a sight!'

The crocodile thought for a moment and then, without saying another word, suddenly dived and swam away.

The hare sat gazing out to sea, very anxious that his plan should work. A whole hour passed, and then, as he was about to abandon hope and return to his form (as a hare's nest is called, for they never use burrows), he saw on the horizon a long strung-out line threshing towards him. It was a multitude of crocodiles, led by his smiling friend, their bodies forming a bridge from his little island of Oki back to the mainland of Inaba. No sooner did the leader's snout touch the

25

beach than the hare called out:

'How splendid you all look! I did not believe it possible. How many of you can there possibly be? I shall have to count you all, and to do this properly I shall, with your permission, jump lightly on to each of your backs until I reach the last of you beautiful creatures on the beach far across the sea. Now keep in a good straight line while I start to count.'

So the hare hopped off the island on to the back of the first of the crocodiles, then on to the next and the next and the next, counting as he jumped from one to the other.

'Please keep quite still! One, two, three, four, five, six, seven, eight . . . .'

Further and further across the crocodile bridge the cunning little hare advanced. He felt perfectly safe for to keep the line straight each crocodile was forced to grip the end of the tail of the creature in front of him so there was no way any of them could take a snap at our friend the hare.

Thus it was that he walked dry-pawed right across to the mainland of Inaba while still pretending to keep up the count.

'One hundred and thirty-seven, one hundred and thirty-eight . . . .'

With a final jump he was on the shore and it was then he made an all-but fatal mistake. He turned in triumph and shouted with a laugh:

'Stupid idiots! I've tricked you! I made you make a bridge, and now I'm on dry land! 'Bye 'bye! 'Bye 'bye! I've made a fool of all of you! 'Bye 'bye! 'Bye 'bye!'

Then the hare turned to run across the shore to the green fields beyond, but stopped in horror at seeing a clutch of very angry-looking crocodiles advancing across the sand towards him. They were the ones not needed to complete the bridge and had waited there for the rest to disperse. In seconds they had formed a circle round the hare, nipping him with their teeth and pulling out mouthfuls of fur.

'Spare me, Mr Crocodiles! Spare me! I'm sorry! I'm sorry!'

But the crocodiles continued pulling out his fur until the poor hare was completely naked. Then they moved down to the sea and swam out of sight.

The hare was now in a pitiful plight. All his beautiful white fur had been pulled out and his bare little body was quivering with pain. All he could do was to lie there on the sand and weep over the misfortune that his own impudence had brought about. If only he had thanked the crocodiles instead of calling them fools!

It was at that moment that a file of men approached, all of them displaying the emblems which marked them as sons of the Emperor. Seeing the hare lying on the sand crying, they stopped to ask what was the matter.

'I've had a fight with some crocodiles and I lost!'

'A fight with some crocodiles? You—a little hare!'

'I did my best, but they beat me and pulled out all my fur.'

The men laughed together then whispered to each other. The eldest, a nasty-looking person who was often cruel to animals, came forward and said that he knew of an immediate cure for the hare's distress.

'Go down and bathe in the sea. Then sit on the beach in the wind and your fur will be back in no time at all!'

Then he and his companions walked away laughing, turning round as they watched the little hare rolling about in the waves, the men laughing even more as they disappeared from sight.

At last the hare came out of the sea and sat where the wind blew hardest. Then, as the salt dried on his body, his skin became drawn and hardened and the pain was worse than ever. The men had cruelly tricked him and all he could do was roll about on the sand and cry with pain.

At that moment the youngest of the Emperor's sons came in sight, having fallen far behind his brothers as they had made him carry most of their baggage. He had a truly kind and compassionate heart and the sight of the little hare, naked and caked with salt, almost brought tears to his eyes.

'You poor little creature. What on earth has happened to bring you to this terrible state?'

But the hare, remembering that he had been deceived by a human only minutes before, did not answer but continued to squeal and cry

with pain.

The youngest son knelt down and tried to comfort him.

'I see all your fur has been pulled out and that your skin is quite bare and covered with salt. Who could have treated you so cruelly?'

When the hare heard these kind words he trusted the man and, encouraged by his gentle manner, the little creature told him all that had happened. He kept nothing back, but told him frankly how he had played a trick on the crocodiles and how he had jeered at them for their stupidity.

When the hare had finished his story the Emperor's son was full of pity towards him, and said:

'I am very sorry for all you have suffered, but a lot of it was your own fault. If you had not been nasty to the crocodiles and deceived them and jeered at them you would still have your lovely white coat of fur.'

'I know,' answered the hare, 'and I have truly repented of my sins and I shall never use deceit again, this I swear!'

'Do you really mean that?'

Between his sobs of pain the hare nodded his head.

'Then,' said the Emperor's son, 'I'll cure your ills and let you have your white coat back again. Now listen carefully. Go to that pond of fresh water and wash and rinse yourself in it until every trace of salt is gone. Do you understand?'

'Yes, sir, I do.'

'Good. After that, pick a large bunch of those *kaba* flowers growing over there, spread them on the ground and roll yourself on them. You will soon be covered in pollen and this will cause your fur to grow again. Now, off you go!'

The poor little naked hare crawled towards the pond of fresh spring water and gradually lowered his body beneath its surface. As the salt was washed away a look akin to bliss gradually spread across his face. The pain was lessening, the dreadful sting was leaving his body and, although he still lacked his fur, he felt renewed. He rubbed his back and stomach with his paws again and again until the pain was almost gone, but then he began to feel the cold.

Shivering, he crawled across to where the *kaba* flowers bloomed and picked a bunch bigger than himself. He made a carpet on the sand and rolled back and forth across it. To his amazement, even while he was still doing this he could feel his beautiful white fur growing again. All the pain ceased and he felt like a brand new hare! Within minutes he had back his thick coat of snow-white fur and was warm and well again.

Overjoyed at his recovery he ran to where the young man stood smiling, and kneeling at his feet he said:

'Sir, I cannot tell you how grateful I am. I think you are the best and kindest man in the world. It is my earnest wish to do something for you in return. Please ask me anything!'

The Emperor's youngest son smiled and shook his head, telling the hare that he had magical powers himself.

'All I want is to marry the beautiful Princess Yakami, but all my brothers have gone to her castle before me, for I have had to carry this heavy bundle and could not keep up with them. She will have already accepted one of them and given her hand before I arrive there.'

'May I know your name?' asked the hare.

'I am Okuni-nushi, the Emperor's youngest son.'

'Okuni-nushi-san,' said the hare, bowing very low. 'I feel sure that so wise and beautiful a Princess would never give her hand in marriage to any of those cruel and unkind men who sent me into the salt water of the sea. Hurry on! She will be waiting for you!'

Suddenly, there was hope in the eyes of the Emperor's son. Dropping the heavy bundle he hurried off in the direction of the palace.

Just as the hare had said, when he arrived there Okuni-nushi-san found to his joy that all his cruel brothers had been rejected by the Princess, but when she looked upon the youngest brother's face her heart melted and she gave him her hand.

'To you I give myself,' she said shyly, and so they were married and lived happily ever after.

This is the end of the story. Okuni-nushi-san has become a legend in Japan for all his good deeds and is now worshipped as a god in some parts of the land. The hare has become famous as 'The White Hare of Inaba'. But what has become of the crocodiles nobody knows.

My Lord Bag-o'-Rice

In Old Japan, in the far-off days when dragons roamed the land, there lived a brave young warrior named Fujiwara-san who was never happier than when he was waging war against the Emperor's enemies. And this is the story of how he came to change his name.

One day, when travelling alone in the mountains with his bow on his back and his two sharp swords in his belt, he came to the curiously carved bridge of Karashi which spanned one end of the beautiful Lake Biwa. It was a lake famous for the flowering trees which lined its banks and for the snow-capped mountains reflected in its surface.

Fujiwara-san was about to cross the bridge when he noticed that a large serpent was coiled in the middle of the centre arch basking in the warm sunshine. It was the biggest snake he had ever seen, seven or eight metres long at least, and at the young warrior's approach it instantly reared its head. It kept still for a minute then, as Fujiwara-san advanced towards it, it suddenly uncoiled and stretched its length across the bridge in such a way that no one could cross without treading on its scaly body.

Ordinary men would have taken to their heels at so frightening a sight, but Fujiwara-san was no ordinary man. Buckling his sword-belt

33

tighter he strode straight ahead, not pausing for so much as a second as he reached the ugly creature, walking across it with a *crunch! squash! crunch! squash!* before turning and giving it a kick. As he did so it blurted a gush of hot air like a slashed balloon, rapidly becoming smaller and smaller and then disappeared. Where the serpent had been there now crouched a tiny dwarf, a little man of uncertain age who was intent on bowing so low to the young warrior that his head touched the planks of the bridge, not once but three times. Then in a fluting voice the dwarf addressed him in respectful tones, keeping his head held low.

'My Lord! You are a man! A brave and fearless man! I bow my head to you!' And once again his forehead bumped the planks.

Fujiwara-san stood silent, his hand lightly gripping the hilt of the larger of his two swords for trickery was to be expected from any of the magic demons who inhabited this part of the country.

'What will you of me?'

'My Lord, I am the Dragon King of Lake Biwa . . . .'

'Dragon King? You were a serpent just now!'

'I can assume many shapes, My Lord. But please hear me. For many a weary day I have lain here, waiting for one who could avenge me on my bitter and cruel enemy. But all who saw me in my serpent's form were cowards. Each one turned and ran away, though there were those amongst them who called themselves warriors. Cowards, every one! But not you, My Lord! Not you!'

'Speak, dwarf, for I have far to journey!'

'My Lord, I live at the bottom of this deep lake and my enemy is a fearful centipede who dwells near the top of yonder mountain. But it is no ordinary centipede I speak of, for its body can circle the mountain top not once but several times. You smile, My Lord, but what I speak is true.'

'What would you have me do?'

'I beseech you to follow me beneath the waters to my humble dwelling where I will tell you the tale of my woes. Then you can avenge me and in return I pledge to bestow on you magic gifts that no man has had before. Follow where I lead, and do not fear the waters for my

36

powers are strong.'

Fujiwara-san thought for a moment then turned and nodded. He had been in many tighter corners than this one and magic presents did not come his way each day—or any day for that matter.

'Lead me where you will.'

Down went the dwarf to the edge of the lake with the young warrior following close behind. Then into the water, deeper and deeper, with the waves seeming to part to let him through until the surface of the lake was above his head. He took a deep breath and found he could still breathe the freshly scented air of Old Japan as naturally as before. It was as though he walked on dry land.

The bed of the lake sloped gently downwards as the strange pair went deeper and deeper below the surface, the little dwarf leading the way and the tall and gallant warrior with his bow and his swords following, taking only one step to the little creature's four or five, brushing aside fishes that swam too close, his right hand on the hilt of a sword that could cut a man in half at a single savage sweep. Once unsheathed it had to taste blood, either his enemy's or, if that failed, his own.

Then, through a hedge of water-weed, he saw the Dragon King's 'humble abode', a beautiful summer-house of brightly-coloured coral set with precious stones, in a garden of rare and exotic seaweeds and flowering water plants. A guard-of-honour was drawn up to greet them, made up of freshwater crabs each the size of a man, while water-monkeys and newts and monster tadpoles acted the part of the Dragon King's servants.

'Rest here, Oh Mighty Sire, while I order refreshments.' And, still in his guise as a dwarf to show his respect for the young warrior, he pointed to the cushions strewn on the tatami floor. In the centre of the room was a Japanese table with carved legs only inches high, and within minutes its surface was covered with exquisite dishes of the finest foods all served on plates shaped like water-lilies. The smaller dishes mimicked watercress leaves, but were more beautiful than the real ones for they were made of water-green jade lined with shimmering gold. As Fujiwara-san picked up his chopsticks he saw they were of a rare petrified wood like black ivory, while the wine they drank was vintage *sake*, a rice-wine of surpassing flavour.

So the young warrior and the dwarf sat cross-legged on the green tatami floor feasting while the sound of lutes and of the sweet-toned *shamisen* charmed their ears.

'I have lived in this lake for many years,' said the Dragon King, 'and I am blessed with a large family of children and grandchildren. But for some time past we have lived in terror, for the monster centipede discovered our home and night after night it comes and carries off one of my family. With all my magic I am still powerless to stop it. My only hope is to seek the powers of a brave human being, a very brave human being. My hopes now rest in you, My Lord.'

And so the dwarf went on, while Fujiwara-san was lulled into a restful sleepiness as the dreadful deeds of the centipede were recounted—the lake polluted time and again, his own and human children devoured, the summer-house wrecked more than once and the countryside terrorised for miles around.

At last the dwarf fell silent and the young warrior was just dozing off when above the sound of the music came the echo of distant thuds. Not one, but many, the noise becoming ever louder as the musicians clutched their instruments in fear and swam rapidly away.

'Rise quickly, I beg you! It's coming! The centipede is coming!'

Instantly Fujiwara-san was on his feet, his long-bow grasped in his hand. He found he could see as clearly through the water as he could through air, the distant mountain standing out against the sky as the thuds increased in violence until it seemed a whole continent was in

motion. The thudding and crashing was deafening in his ears, and, as the danger drew nearer, the young warrior could see the monstrous centipede. It was unbelievably huge, an enormous creature a mile or more long. On either side of it there seemed to be a row of a thousand men with lanterns in their hands. Then, as its huge head reached the shores of the lake, Fujiwara-san realised that what he had taken for lines of marching men with lanterns were, in fact, the giant centipede's thousand pairs of feet, all of them glistening and glinting with the sticky poison that oozed from every pore.

There was no time to be lost for the monstrous creature was about to enter the lake. Quick as a flash the young warrior fitted one of his three arrows to the string of the bow, a bow so big and strong that it would have taken three ordinary men to pull it. Taking careful aim with the string at full stretch he let the arrow fly.

He was not one ever to miss his mark, and, sure enough, the arrow struck clean in the middle of the centipede's forehead. To Fujiwara-san's amazement there was a clang and the shaft rebounded! It was as though the monster's head was made of brass!

A second time did our hero take his bow and shoot, and a second

time did the arrow find its mark only to glance harmlessly off and ricochet away into the trees.

He had only one arrow left in his quiver. As he fitted the notch to the bow-string he remembered being told by his father when a small boy that centipedes could be killed by human spit. He recalled that he had gone straight out into the garden to spit on one. Sure enough, it had instantly coiled itself into a ball and died. The one in the garden was a few centimetres long, but the beast before him stretched for more than a mile. Would the spittle work?

It had to! It was his only hope! Holding the arrow-head close to his mouth Fujiwara-san spat on it, then let fly the missile just as the centipede raised the first pair of its thousand legs to enter Lake Biwa. Once again the arrow hit the monster in the centre of its forehead, but this time instead of rebounding it penetrated so deeply as to come out at the back of the creature's head. Instantly the centipede reared itself high in the sky, then quivering along its entire length, it keeled over and fell with a crash that shook the earth for miles around. People in villages leagues away rushed out of their houses thinking that an earthquake had taken place and then watched in wonderment as a

huge cloud of dust rose into the heavens from the direction of the lake. The centipede was dead, but for an hour or more its feet still glowed and lit up the shoreline. Then one by one they too dimmed and died.

As the light in the last pair of feet was extinguished Fujiwara-san was suddenly whisked off his feet to be transported in seconds back to his own castle. When he opened his eyes it was to find himself in the courtyard surrounded by presents all of which bore labels inscribed with the words 'From your very grateful dwarf'.

The first and much the largest was a dome-shaped bronze bell which our young warrior caused to be hung up in the local temple which contained the tombs of his forbears, for every Japanese man and woman honours the memory of their ancestors.

He was very pleased with the second of the Dragon King's presents, a magic sword whose edge could as easily cut through stone or steel as it could a floating feather. With this and his third present, a suit of armour which no arrow could penetrate, there was no way he could be vanquished by jealous enemies.

Label number four was tied to a bolt of the most expensive and finest silk, a roll of material which had the ability to change colour and design as the mood took him, and which, no matter how many times his wife cut off large or small pieces for yet another kimono or for a new court dress for her Master, never became any less. The roll always remained the same length as though it had not been touched, so that Fujiwara-san often had clothes made for poor people and their children and his name was blessed throughout the land.

But it was the fifth present that gave him the most joy. It was a large bag of best quality rice, which, though the family scooped measures from it every day for meals for themselves and their trusty retainers, remained always full. It never diminished in quantity so that Fujiwara-san was always able to feed the poor and needy.

Within weeks he was being referred to as 'My Lord Bag-o'-Rice', words spoken with the utmost respect and always with a low bow of the head. He and his family were loved throughout Old Japan and he finally died a venerated saint and a rich and happy man.

43

The Tongue-cut Sparrow

Many years ago in Old Japan there lived a farmer and his wife in their little wooden house deep in a forest of trees and bamboo. The husband, Sangiro-san was a kind-hearted, hard-working old fellow, but the wife was a bad-tempered crosspatch, constantly nagging and a regular shrew in all her ways. She seemed always to be grumbling about something or other and gave her husband little peace either by day or night.

Over the years he had gradually become indifferent to much of what she had to say, and most of the day he was out of her sight working in the fields or in the forest. They had no children, but for his amusement he had caught and tamed a little sparrow. He grew to love the tiny bird just as if it had been his very own child. When he came back at night after his hard day's work it gave him great pleasure to pet the sparrow, to talk to her and teach her little tricks. Often he would open her cage and let her fly about the room, and when supper-time came he always saved some of the choicest tit-bits to feed to his little playmate.

Then came the day when the old man went off to collect logs and kindling wood while his wife grumbled about having to wash clothes all day. She discovered that her starch bowl was quite empty, although the previous afternoon she had prepared enough for the day's washing. Who could have used or stolen it, she asked herself? At that moment down flew the pet sparrow, and bowing his little feathered head, a trick taught her by her master, the pretty creature chirped and said:

'Forgive me! It was I who have taken your starch. I had no idea what it was and thought my master had left it there for me to eat. I ate it all. If I have made a mistake I beg you to forgive me! Tweet, tweet, tweet!'

The old woman had always disliked the sparrow, knowing the pleasure the bird gave to her husband. She had often quarrelled with him over it, saying it was a dirty bird that caused her much extra work, so now she was secretly delighted at being able to punish the poor little creature. All this time the sparrow perched with its wings outspread and its head bowed to show how sorry she was at her mistake, while the nasty old woman cursed the bird for its behaviour.

'Please forgive me, my gentle mistress! Please forgive me!'

'Gentle mistress is it! I'll show you how gentle I am!'

Reaching for her scissors she snatched up the sparrow and cut off the end of the poor little creature's tongue!

'That was the tongue which ate my starch! Now you may see what it's like to be without it!'

With these dreadful words she threw the sparrow out of the door, then, still grumbling, went back indoors to make some more rice-paste starch, spreading the starched garments on boards to dry in the sun instead of ironing them, as was the custom in those days.

In the early evening the old man came home, bowed down by the weight of the logs and sticks he carried. As he neared his gate he was surprised not to be greeted by his little sparrow, for she would watch from the window for her master's homecoming, flying out chirping with pleasure to alight on his shoulder. There she would ruffle out her feathers to show her joy. But tonight the old man was very disappointed, for not even the shadow of his dear little friend was to be seen.

Something was wrong—he could feel it in his bones, and he

hastened his steps, kicking off his sandals as he reached the verandah. Still no sparrow was to be seen, and he felt sure that his wife, in one of her tempers, had shut the sparrow up in her cage. He called out anxiously: 'Where is Suzume-san today?'

'Your sparrow? Don't ask me.'

'She *must* be somewhere!'

'I don't know where she is. Now I come to think of it, I haven't seen the wretched bird all afternoon. The ungrateful little devil has probably flown away and left you after all your petting.'

But the old man had noticed that his wife would not, or could not, look him in the eyes, and his suspicions hardened into certainties. He questioned her unceasingly, again and again, following her around the house insisting that she must know what had happened to his pet. Finally, his wife broke down and confessed all that she had done. She told him how the sparrow had eaten the rice-paste she had specially made to starch their clothes, and that when the sparrow confessed she had lost her temper and cut out its tongue before throwing the bird out of the door. She had watched it fly off into the forest—and good riddance!

'How could you be so cruel? Oh! how could you be so cruel?' was all the old man could bring himself to say. He shed many tears as he thought of the fate of his dear little Suzume-san, and how she would never be able to chirp her little greeting to him again.

'What can I do? I must find her!'

But darkness had now fallen so there could be no searching that night. As he wiped away his tears with the sleeve of his cotton kimono he vowed that the whole of tomorrow would be spent seeking his little friend.

The next morning he was awake and about as dawn broke, snatching a mouthful of breakfast before hastening out into the woods in search of his dear little sparrow. At every clump of bamboo he would stop and cry: 'Where, oh where, is my tongue-cut sparrow? Where does my tongue-cut sparrow stay?'

All the morning and all through to early afternoon he cried the same phrases, not even stopping to eat his lunch of dried squid and

rice-balls. At last he found himself at the edge of a large bamboo wood. Bamboo groves are the favourite haunts of Japanese sparrows, and there, sure enough, at the edge of this wood he saw his own dear sparrow waiting to welcome him. The old farmer fell to his knees with joy, then rose and ran forward to greet his little pet. She bowed her head and performed a number of tricks he had taught her, and—wonder of wonders—she could talk just as before!

The old man told her how sorry he was at what his wicked wife had done to her, then inquired after her tongue, wondering how on earth she was able to speak and chirp without it. At once the sparrow opened her beak and showed him that a new tongue had grown in the place of the old one.

'Don't think any more of the past, I beg you. I am quite well now.'

It would be difficult to exaggerate the old man's joy, for he realised for the first time that the little bird he had cherished for so long was a fairy, and a good fairy at that! He forgot all his own troubles, he forgot how tired he was, for he had found his lost sparrow. Instead of being ill, perhaps even dying, she was as well as she had ever been, and in

place of her severed tongue there was a brand new one. She was without a sign of the ill-treatment she had received from his wife, and, best of all, she was undoubtedly a fairy!

The sparrow asked him to follow her, and she flew between the clumps of bamboo, pausing now and then to allow him to catch up. Suddenly they were in a clearing in the centre of the wood and there stood one of the most beautiful houses the old farmer had ever seen. As the sparrow entered the porch her magical powers became evident for she assumed the form of a princess, dressed in a wonderful silk kimono, though her face still had birdlike qualities. The old man quickly kicked off his sandals and followed her inside, gasping with astonishment at the beauty of the rooms. They were built of the whitest of woods, with soft cream-coloured mats which took the place of carpets, while the cushions the Sparrow Princess brought him to sit on were made of the finest silk. In the alcoves stood precious vases decorated with flying cranes and other birds, while the lacquer boxes were of the most skilful workmanship.

The Sparrow Princess led the old farmer to the place of honour, taking her own place at a respectful distance. She thanked him again for all the many kindnesses he had shown her, bowing low to show her gratitude. This done, she called in her daughters, robed in their dainty silk gowns, each bowing low in turn. Then they left, to return with old-fashioned silver trays set with all kinds of delicious foods which they placed before him. He pinched himself to make sure he was awake and that all this was not just a dream.

Never had Sangiro-san used his chopsticks to better effect. 'Hunger is the best sauce!' he told his hostess, while the Sparrow Princess's daughters performed a *Suzume-odori* or 'Sparrows' Dance' to amuse their guest.

At last the meal was over and never had the old man enjoyed himself so much. The hours flew by too quickly in this lovely spot, with all these fairy sparrows to wait on him and to feast him and to dance before him. But night was coming on and darkness reminded him that he had to leave for home.

'I thank you for your generous hospitality to a humble farmer, but I must now take my leave. I have far to go.'

The Sparrow Princess begged him to stay and rest for several days, but sadly he shook his head. He must return to his bad-tempered wife and to his work. His crops needed constant attention for the old man and his wife were very poor people and needed to put by enough to live through the coming winter. So he must say goodbye, but now that he knew where his little pet lived he would often visit them, he promised.

When the Sparrow Princess saw that she could not persuade the old man to stay longer, she gave an order to some of her servants. They at once brought in two boxes, one large and the other small. These they placed before the farmer and the Sparrow Princess asked him to choose whichever he liked for a present. At first he protested that he had already received gifts enough, but when she insisted he said he would choose the small box.

'I am now too old and feeble to carry the big and heavy one. I will choose the small one. It will be easier for me to carry.'

Then the sparrows all helped him to strap it to his back and bade him goodbye with many bows. They entreated him to come again whenever he had the time. And so they parted happily.

When after some hours the old man reached home he found his wife even more bad-tempered than usual.

'Where the devil have you been? How dare you stay out so late!'

He tried to pacify her by showing her the box and relating all his adventures, and it was not long before her curiosity got the better of her.

'Open it, then! Let's see what's inside!'

To their utter astonishment they found the box filled to the brim with gold and silver coins, jewels, and many other precious things. The tatami mats of their little cottage sparkled and glittered as they tipped the contents of the box across the floor, and the old man was overjoyed at the sight of the riches which were now his. The sparrow's gift was beyond his greatest expectations, a gift that would enable him to give up work and live in ease and comfort for the rest of his days.

'Thanks to my good little sparrow! Thanks to my dear little sparrow!' he cried and, although the Japanese seldom show emotion, tears of gratitude welled up in Sangiro-san's eyes.

Within a few hours, after her rapture at their good fortune had subsided, his cantankerous old wife started to reproach him for not choosing the larger of the two boxes.

'You say it was four times as large and four times as heavy! What did it matter if it took you two whole days to get it here? Think of the wealth you have let slip through your idle fingers! You must have been mad to make such an idiotic choice!'

'But we've plenty here, dear. There is more than enough gold and silver to keep us happy for the rest of our days. Be content!'

'You silly old man!' she screamed at him. 'We might have had four times as much gold and silver as this. You are a silly old fool!' And she stalked off to bed beside herself with anger.

Her husband bitterly regretted ever having told her of the choice he had made, or of having mentioned the larger of the two boxes, but it was too late. His greedy old wife, not content with the good luck which had so unexpectedly befallen them, and which she so little deserved, made up her mind in bed that night that she was going to get more.

She, too, was up at dawn, and set off to find the bamboo forest, following the directions her husband had revealed to her when he first arrived home. When, later, Sangiro-san awoke and found her gone he was filled with foreboding and in his anger hurried after her. But by now she was miles away and he sadly turned back and retraced his steps.

Ever since the Sparrow Princess had returned home in distress and bleeding from the mouth, her family and friends had utterly condemned the old woman.

'How could she? How could she inflict such a dreadful punishment for such a trifling offence as that of eating some rice-paste by mistake?'

They all loved the old man who was always so kind and good and patient under all his troubles, but the old woman they disliked intensely and they were determined, if ever they had the chance, to punish her as she deserved. They had not long to wait!

It was some hours after leaving home that Sangiro-san's wife at last found the grove of bamboo, and now she stood before it crying: 'Where is the tongue-cut sparrow's house? Where is the tongue-cut sparrow's house?'

She pushed her way through the clumps of bamboo until she glimpsed the eaves of the beautiful house in its setting in the clearing. Without more ado she hurried to the porch, kicking off her sandals as she hastened to reach the door. She knocked loudly, crying out at the same time: 'I know this is the tongue-cut sparrow's house, so open the door!'

The servants inside could hardly believe her rudeness, but at a nod from the Sparrow Princess they slid open the door and let the old woman in.

Hardly permitting herself the courtesy of a bow, and with no word of apology for her cruel acts, she came straight to the point.

'You need not trouble to entertain me as you did my old man. I have travelled many miles to get the box he so stupidly left behind. When you have handed over the big box I shall take my leave. It is all I have come for.'

The Sparrow Princess bowed.

'I thought you might have some words to explain your past actions?'

The old woman shook her head.

'Bring me the box and I'll be off.'

Again the Sparrow Princess bowed.

'Be it as you will.'

At a word to her servants they left the room, returning immediately with the large box which Sangiro's wife almost pulled from their hands before hoisting it on her back. Without even a word of thanks she was off back through the bamboo wood as she hurried homewards.

The box was so heavy she could walk only slowly and despite her anxiety to get home quickly to open it she was forced to stop and rest every few minutes, sitting on the box as she recovered her breath. She kept thinking of all the gold and silver and jewels it must contain and when she halted for about the tenth time her greed and curiosity overcame her.

She put the box down again at the side of the path and pulled out the securing bolt of the lock. Then she slowly lifted the heavy lid. She expected to gloat over a positive mine of wealth, but what she actually saw made her almost faint away in fear! As soon as she lifted the lid a

horde of frightful demons leapt out of the box and surrounded her as though they meant to kill her. Not even in nightmares had she ever seen such horrible creatures; the largest of the monsters, with a third eye set in the middle of its forehead, glared at her with it, while other demons with gaping mouths advanced as though to devour her.

With a piercing scream she was on her feet and away as fast as her quaking legs could carry her. She was glad to escape alive and when she finally gasped her way to the door of her home she fell to her knees and with tears running down her face asked her husband's forgiveness. She told him all that had happened to her, and then began to blame the Sparrow Princess for all her troubles.

'Don't blame the sparrow! It is your own greed and wickedness that have brought these calamities on you. I only hope this will be a lesson to you in the future. Now say you're sorry!'

At first his old wife said nothing, and then, in a whisper he could only just hear said the one word—'Sorry.'

'Now say you're sorry to the Sparrow Princess, too!'

'I'm sorry. And I'm sorry I've been so nagging and bad-tempered to you in the past.'

Even though she said it, Sangiro-san's wife could not believe her ears as the words came out. But directly she had finished speaking it was as though a weight had been lifted from her back. She felt happiness and optimism sweep through her and from that day onwards she became a kindly and loving wife to her husband. No doubt it was another of the Sparrow Princess's magic spells, but it certainly worked, for the old farmer and his wife lived happily to the end of their days.

The Adventures of a Fisher Lad

Long, long ago there lived on the coast of Japan in a little fishing village called Mizu-no-ye a young fisherman named Urashima Taro. His father and grandfather had been fishermen before him and their skills had been inherited by Urashima, for he was the most successful fisher on that entire coast and often caught more *bonito* and *tai* fish in a day than his comrades could in a week.

In his village he was renowned for his kind heart, and as a child he would never join in the so-called 'sport' of teasing animals and always did his best to stop his companions being cruel or vicious as children sometimes are.

One soft summer twilight he had just pulled his boat up on the sands of the beach when he noticed a group of young people crowding round something as they laughed and joked. He walked over and was angry to see that they had caught a young turtle and were hitting it and stamping on it, then turning it on its back and kicking it.

'Stop this, at once!'

He turned and picked up the turtle, pushing the children aside and knocking the ringleader of the group off his feet. Instantly each and every one of them took to their heels and fled, leaving Urashima alone with the turtle. The poor little thing was obviously bruised and injured, but its shell was intact and nothing seemed to be broken.

'There, there! You are safe now. I'll see you will come to no more harm.'

And Urashima stroked the turtle's back and carried it tenderly to the edge of the waves. He put it in the water and watched as it slowly waddled out, then started swimming and disappeared.

The next morning Urashima went out as usual in his boat. The weather was fine and the sea and sky were both blue in the tender haze

of the summer morning. He soon passed the other fishing boats and left them behind him until they were lost to sight in the distance. Somehow, he knew not why, he felt unusually happy that morning, and he sang softly to himself as the boat drifted gently over the waves.

Suddenly he was startled to hear his own name called.

'Urashima! Urashima!'

Clear as a bell and soft as the summer wind the name floated over the sea.

He stood up and looked in every direction, being sure that one of his

companion's boats had overtaken him, but gaze as he might over the wide expanse of ocean, there was no sign of any living soul.

'Urashima! Urashima!'

There it was again! He twisted round, knowing that it was no human voice which called his name. Then he saw it! A turtle had come to the side of the boat and was attempting to climb aboard. Urashima realised immediately, by the pattern of its shell, that it was the very same turtle he had rescued only yesterday. He bent over the boat's side and lifted it aboard.

'Well Mr Turtle, was it you that called my name just now?'

The turtle nodded its head several times, and said: 'Yes, it was I. Yesterday in your honourable shadow my life was saved. I have come to offer you my thanks and to tell you how grateful I am for your great kindness in rescuing me.'

'It was nothing.'

'Indeed it was! Tell me, have you ever seen Rin Gin, the palace of the Dragon King of the Sea, Urashima-san?'

The young fisherman shook his head, and said that year after year the sea had been his home, but although he had often heard tell of the Sea King's palace he had never yet set eyes on the wonderful place. It must be very far away, if it existed at all.

The turtle smiled, as only a turtle can.

'You have missed seeing one of the wonders of the world, I can assure you of that. It is one of the most astonishing sights in the whole universe. It is far away at the bottom of the sea, but I will be your guide.'

'I should like to go there, certainly, but I am a human. There is no way that I could breathe under the water, and besides that, your back is far too small for me to ride on.'

Before Urashima could say any more the turtle stopped him, saying: 'I will take care of everything. Trust me. Now, on my back you get for I am determined to repay your kindness.'

When the young fisherman turned to look he was astonished to see that the turtle had grown to human size, and its back was so large that he had no difficulty in putting his arms around its neck and seating himself firmly.

'Here we go!'

There was a splash and Urashima found himself beneath the waves and diving rapidly, yet there was no sense of getting wet and he found that he could breathe as easily as if he had been on dry land.

Deeper and deeper the turtle dived, until at last, in the far distance, a magnificent gate appeared and behind the gate the long, sloping roofs of a huge palace.

'Can you see it, Urashima-san? That is the gate of the Rin Gin Palace.'

'And is that the Sea King's palace beyond the gate?'

'It is, indeed! Now you must dismount and walk with me.'

The turtle went in front and speaking to the gatekeeper said: 'This is Urashima Taro-san, from the country of Japan. I have the honour of bringing him as a visitor to this kingdom. Please show him the way.'

The gatekeeper, who was a species of fish which Urashima-san did not recognise, bowed low and led the way through the gate towards the palace. Red bream, flounders, soles, cuttlefish, and all the chief vassals of the Dragon King of the Sea now came out with courtly bows

to welcome the stranger.

'Urashima-san! Urashima-san! Welcome to the Sea Palace, the home of the Dragon King of the Sea. Thrice welcome are you, having come from such a distant country. Please follow us this way.'

Urashima, being only a poor fisher lad, did not know how to behave in a palace, so he bowed to everyone in turn and followed where they led. When they finally reached the portals a beautiful Princess with her attendant maidens came out to welcome him. She was more beautiful than any human he had ever seen, and was robed in flowing garments of red and soft green painted by the seaweeds. Golden threads glimmered through the folds of her gown. Her long black hair streamed over her shoulders and when she spoke her voice sounded like music over the waters.

Urashima-san was lost in wonder as he gazed at her and could not speak. Then he remembered that he had forgotten to bow, but before he could do so the Princess took him by the hand and led him to a beautiful hall, and to the seat of honour.

'Urashima-san, it gives me the greatest pleasure to welcome you to my father's kingdom,' said the Princess. 'Yesterday you rescued and set free a turtle, and I have brought you here to thank you again for saving my life, for I was that turtle. Now if you like you can live here for ever in the land of eternal youth, where summer never dies and where sorrow never comes.' She looked coyly down and blushed. 'If you will, I will be your bride and we can live happily for ever and ever.'

As Urashima listened to her sweet words and gazed upon her lovely face, his heart was filled with a great joy. Could it all be just a dream?

'You do me too much honour, Princess. Thank you a thousand times. There is nothing I would wish for better than to stay here for ever with you.'

While he was speaking a shoal of fishes appeared, all dressed in ceremonial robes which trailed behind them like floating shawls. Each bore a coral tray, piled high with delicacies of exotic foods, plus the rice-balls and seaweed that were the staple diet of the Japan Urashima had come from. Within minutes a marvellous feast was set before the bride and bridegroom. The marriage itself was celebrated with dazzling splendour, and throughout the Sea King's dominions there was great rejoicing. As soon as the young pair had pledged themselves by each drinking a wedding cup of wine, three times three, there was a cheer from the thronged hall and congratulations were showered on them. Urashima had never felt happier and never in his whole life had he sat down to such a splendid feast.

When, after many hours, the meal was over, the bride asked the bridegroom if he would like to walk through the palace to see all there was to be seen. Then, the happy young fisherman, following in the footsteps of the Sea King's daughter, was shown all the wonders of the enchanted land where youth never ages. Even more than the palace itself, the garden with which it was surrounded seemed to Urashima an enchanted land. Here was to be seen, at one and the same time, all four of the seasons. If you looked to the east, plum and cherry trees were seen in full bloom, the nightingales sang sweetly in the white and pink avenues of flowers and butterflies flitted between the branches. Looking to the south all the trees were clothed in green, and amongst the flowers it was flaming June; a profusion of colour! Looking to the west, the maples were ablaze in autumnal browns and oranges, and banks of chrysanthemums bloomed to perfection. Finally, he looked to the north, and for a moment Urashima's eyes were blinded. The ground was silver-white with snow, the trees and bamboos were stiff with icicles, and frost sparkled like diamonds from every vantage point.

Each day there were new joys and new wonders, and so great was his happiness that he quite forgot the home he had left behind, and his parents, and his friends in the village of Mizu-no-ye. Three whole days passed without him even thinking of his old life in Japan, but suddenly he awoke on the morning of the fourth day and felt strong pangs of homesickness. What must his parents be thinking? They would be sure to think he had drowned at sea and their grief must be great at the loss of their young son and heir. He must return to his village at once!

He hurried off to find his beautiful young wife and bowing low before her he told her of his intention.

'You have been kinder to me than any words can tell, Otohime-san. But my parents will think I am dead. I must return to them immediately.'

The Princess began to weep and asked him if all was not well with him here in the Rin Gin Palace.

'I understand your reasons, but why the haste? Stay with me just a few more days. Please, Urashima-san!'

Again her husband shook his head.

'I must go to see my parents, but I promise you I will not stay for more than a few days. I will come back to you as soon as I can and I promise you I will not be long.'

'Then,' said the Princess sorrowfully, 'there is nothing more that I can say. I shall give you this gift as a token of my love. Please take it back with you to Japan.'

She handed him a beautiful lacquer box tied about with a silken cord from which hung tassels of red silk. Urashima protested that she had given him too many gifts already, but when she insisted he said he would do as she said.

'What is in the box, may I ask?'

'This is the Box of the Jewel Hand,' answered Otohime-san, 'and it contains something very precious. You must swear to me that you will not open the box whatever happens. Promise me this immediately, for if you do open it something very dreadful will happen. Now promise me!'

And Urashima promised that whatever happened he would never, never, *never* open the box.

Bidding his wife a fond goodbye he made his way down to the seashore, the Princess and her attendants following him. There he found a large turtle whose back he quickly mounted and he was carried away across the wide sea into the east. He waved back to Otohime-san until she was lost to sight and soon after the palace itself could no longer be seen. Then he turned his face to the east and eagerly awaited the rising of the blue hills on the horizon.

At long last the turtle carried him into the bay he knew so well and to the shore from which he had set out. Urashima jumped down from its back as it turned to swim back to the distant palace.

The shoreline was the same and so were the hills in the distance, but all the people—the people he knew so well, the people he had grown up with—why did he recognise no one? Not one single face did he know! Many turned to stare curiously at him as they would a stranger and even the way they spoke seemed slightly different.

Quickly he strode off to his parents' house, only to stop dead as it came into view. There was a house on the spot, certainly, but it was entirely different from the house he had grown up in. A great fear began to grip Urashima, but, as he reached the gate, he forced himself to call out in a voice that trembled:

'Father! Father—I'm back!'

The door slid back and a total stranger stood there, then went to close the door again.

'Excuse me! Excuse me!' Urashima called out, so that the door was slid open again. 'I'm Urashima Taro and I've been away a few days. Where have my parents gone whom I left here?'

The stranger looked bewildered, saying that he and his family had lived there for over twenty years.

'And you say you are Urashima Taro-san? There has never been a Urashima Taro in this village that I know of, and I know everyone here.'

'But this is my village! This is Mizu-no-ye! Why does everything look the same but very different? What has happened while I've been away?'

The stranger shook his head, then slowly a smile spread across his face.

'This is a joke! I know it now! I am the Keeper of the Village Records at the shrine, and you, sir, must have read about Urashima Taro, as I now remember reading. He was a well-known fisher lad and was lost at sea—but that was about three hundred years ago!'

Urashima felt his face growing white and a fearful anxiety chilled his body.

'Please! Please! You must not joke with me. I really am Urashima Taro and until a few days ago I lived at this exact spot.'

The stranger's face grew grave again and he drew back a pace.

'You may think you are Urashima Taro, but he has been dead three hundred years. Please bring this house no harm, for I believe you to be his ghost come back to visit his old home.'

'Ghost! I'm no ghost! I am a living man—do you not see my feet?' And he stamped them on the ground, raising a small cloud of dust, knowing that Japanese legend has it that ghosts have no feet and merely glide along.

But the man persisted, shaking his head and repeating that Urashima Taro lived and died some three hundred years ago.

'The village chronicles have his death recorded.'

Urashima was lost in bewilderment. He turned again to look around him and the more he looked the more puzzled he became. Something in the appearance of every single house and landmark was different from what he remembered when he went away and the awful feeling came over him that perhaps what the man said was true.

He now felt he was in a dream and that the few days he had spent in the Sea King's palace beyond the sea had not been days at all. Time must be different there: what he had thought of as days must have been hundreds of years and in that time his parents had died and all the people he had ever known. There was no use in staying here any longer. He must get back to his beautiful wife in the Rin Gin Palace.

Urashima made his way back to the beach, carrying in his hand the box the Princess had given him. As he reached the waves he paused.

67

Which was the way? How was he to return to her for there was no turtle in sight and might never be. He could not find the way alone.

Suddenly, he thought of the precious box, the Box of the Jewel Hand, but the Princess had told him that he must not open it and he had given her his promise.

'But now that I have no home, now that I have lost everything,' he said to himself, 'now that all that was dear to me here is lost and my heart grows thin with sadness, surely at such a time what is in the box will be of the greatest help to me in my misfortunes.'

He let his fingers play with the cords which secured the lid, then took his hand away, knowing how earnestly his wife had warned him.

Then he began to persuade himself again, telling himself that if he was ever to find his way back to the Rin Gin Palace he *must* seek the help of whatever was inside the Box of the Jewel Hand.

'I feel sure I'll find something inside that will show me the way back to my beautiful Princess. I have no other hope. Yes, yes, I will open the box and look in!'

Slowly, very slowly, he untied the red silk cords which bound the lid, letting them drop to the sand. But he still kept the lid pressed down. Should he or shouldn't he? Then slowly, very slowly, he gradually raised the lacquered lid.

And what did he find? Strange to say only a beautifully scented purple cloud rose out of the box in three soft wisps. For an instant it covered his face as though loth to go, then it slowly floated away like vapour over the sea.

Urashima, who until that moment had been a strong and handsome youth in his early twenties, suddenly became very, very old. His back doubled up with age, his hair turned snowy white and his face became creased with a multitude of wrinkles. He was an old, old man.

Then he keeled over on his side and fell dead on the beach.

Poor Urashima! Had he only kept his word until sunset a magic turtle would have appeared to transport him back to his lovely wife. But he had disobeyed her and ignored her warning and the gods had punished him.

The Old Man Who Made Dead Trees Bloom

Long ago there lived an old man and his wife who were very poor indeed. They had only a tiny plot of land to grow their food, yet they were happy and contented, their only sorrow being the knowledge that their marriage had not been blessed with any children.

But they had a dog named Shiro and on him they lavished all their affection. Now Shiro in Japanese means 'white' and they had given their pet that name because of his colour and even in the dusk of evening they could see him fields away.

Shiro always went with his master when he worked in the fields, staying out all day and returning with him to share part of his frugal supper of dried squid and rice-balls and vegetables. When the old man, who was called Sentaro-san, said, 'Chin, chin!' the dog would sit up and beg and be given tasty morsels. Unfortunately, the old couple's neighbours were a cruel and bad-tempered man and his wife and when the dog went to the verandah of their house to beg, he was chased and beaten and even on his master's land sometimes had stones thrown at him.

One fine evening in early spring the old man took his wife a long walk to see the beauty of the cherry blossom. Shiro trotted along ahead of them through the woods, then suddenly stopped and started to scratch the ground with both his fore feet. 'What is it, old dog?' said his master. 'What has Shiro found for us, then?' But still the dog continued to scratch and as the old couple bent down to look they saw the glint of coins. It was a buried hoard of gold and Sentaro-san excitedly scooped handful after handful so that the sleeves of his wife's kimono were weighed down with the treasure. But when their bad-tempered neighbours heard of their good fortune they were wild with jealousy though they tried not to show this, pretending to congratulate sincerely the old man and his wife while all the time plotting how they could benefit themselves. Finally, after much pleading, Sentaro-san agreed to lend them his dog for a short time and despite its barking it was led away on a chain.

No sooner did the wicked couple reach their home than the husband took up his spade. Then the two of them dragged poor Shiro out into the woods until they reached a tall yenoki tree. Here the man threatened the dog with his spade, saying:

'You found gold coins for your master, now you must find some for me! Come on! Get on with it!'

Shiro, who was an intelligent dog, at once began to scratch the ground beneath the tree much to the delight of his keeper holding the chain. Pushing the animal aside the wicked neighbour began immediately to dig, shovelling soil and leaves and twigs violently backwards all over his wife's feet. Deeper and deeper he dug and a particularly foul smell began to come from the hole. He had unearthed a dump of rotting rubbish!

The man's temper, already frayed, at once gave way.

'I'll teach you to trick me!' he screamed, and with one blow of his spade he struck the poor dog dead. His wife, who obeyed him in everything, seemed shocked, but at her husband's command she picked up the dead dog and threw it into the hole he had made. The wicked neighbour stalked off back home, leaving her to fill in the grave.

Several days went by and Sentaro-san and his wife missed their dear Shiro more and more, until finally the old man called at his neighbour's house and asked where his dog was. Almost without any apology he was told quite brutally that Shiro was dead, killed he was told, because of the dog's bad behaviour.

'How could you do such a thing to such a poor sweet creature?' and the old man let a tear fall as he put his hands to his face.

'You'll find the grave under the yenoki tree.'

Sadly Sentaro-san stood at the fresh turned earth, then, in memory of his faithful friend he cut down the tree and carted it home to his wife. Out of the trunk he made a large wooden pot, telling his wife she could use it to pound the rice in and that each time they used it they would think of Shiro. The old lady next day did as she was bid, only to call out to her husband in amazement that the rice flour was increasing of its own accord and cakes were being turned out of the pot as though by an invisible hand! Then they realised that this was Shiro's way of saying thank you for their faithful love of him.

Their greedy neighbours, hearing of this new piece of good luck, were filled with envy as before. In a few days they called on the old couple and begged to borrow the wooden pot, pretending that they wished to honour the memory of the dog Shiro and stating that they were truly sorry for having killed their neighbour's pet. This was quite untrue, of course, and merely a trick to gain possession of the wonderful wooden bowl. They pleaded again and again until at last Sentaro-san gave in. He and his wife were too kind-hearted to refuse, especially when their cunning neighbours promised to return the magic vessel in a day or two. So the envious couple carried off the pot to their own house. But they never brought it back!

Once again the old man was forced to walk over to his neighbour's house to ask if he might have back that which, out of the goodness of his heart, he had loaned. He found his wicked companion sitting by a big fire made from pieces of wood, while on the grass nearby were what appeared to be sections of Sentaro-san's wooden bowl. In answer to his enquiry the man scowled and continued chopping and throwing pieces of the bowl on the fire.

'Fancy wanting that stupid pot back! All the rice my wife put in it turned bad within seconds. We both hate the thing and now it's burned!'

The good old man looked very sad, shaking his head at his neighbour's wickedness.

'If you had told me you wanted rice cakes my wife would have given you all you could possibly carry. Now please give me the ashes of the wooden bowl you have burned. I wish to keep them in remembrance of my dog.'

'Ashes? You must be mad! Help yourself, you silly old fool!'

Sentaro-san had to wait for over an hour for the fire to cool, but finally he had a basket full to the brim with ashes, and, being careful to sweep the ground clean, he left for home.

It was later that year, just before the winter snows, that the old man looked at the bare branches of the plum and cherry trees that lined his garden and sighed deeply. How often had he and his dear dog Shiro walked together in those same woods? Sadly he took down the sealed wooden box that contained the ashes and, with it under his arm, he walked slowly out to stand amongst the trees. Something, he knew not what, told him to break the seal and open the box. There were the dull grey ashes just as before, but as he stood with the open box a sudden puff of wind sent a thin dusting over the trees nearest to him. Then a miracle happened! Each tree the ashes had touched burst immediately into full bloom! It was as though spring had arrived, each bough and branch was hung with sweetly scented blossom. Sentaro-san stood rooted in amazement, then, carefully resealing the lid of the box, he hurried back to tell his wife.

The story of the old man's garden soon spread far and wide and people came from miles away to stand and gaze at the wonderful sight. A little more ashes next morning on shrubs and borders had brought a fresh blaze of colour and soon it seemed as though the whole of Japan was beating a path to the old couple's door.

A few weeks later Sentaro-san received a summons to attend at the Palace of the Shogun in far away Kyoto, and His Serene Highness actually sent a ceremonial palanquin carried by six strong men to transport him there. One of the Shogun's favourite cherry trees in the palace gardens had withered and died, but having heard of the

wonderful old man whose garden bloomed in winter he now hoped that the tree could be revived.

The Shogun was impatiently waiting his arrival and no sooner did the palanquin appear than Sentaro-san was taken to the throne-room and into the presence of His Highness.

'Are you the old man who can make withered trees flower, even out of season?'

Sentaro-san bowed very low.

'I am that old man, Your Highness.'

The Shogun nodded.

'You must make the dead cherry tree in my garden blossom by means of your famous ashes and I shall look on.'

They all went into the garden, the Shogun accompanied by his many retainers and his ladies-in-waiting, all of them excited and whispering and giggling behind their fans.

'There is the tree. Now let me see your magic.'

The old man tucked his kimono into his sash and made ready to climb the tree, the box containing the ashes under his arm. It was a very large tree, some said over a hundred years old, divided into two great branches from which had sprouted dozens of smaller ones. All were withered and gnarled, with not so much as a leaf or bud or

blossom to be seen.

Everyone watched with baited breath as Sentaro-san climbed into the fork of the tree and carefully opened his precious box. Tipping some of the ashes into his hand he blew gently first this way and then the other. A gasp came from the crowd of onlookers and then something very like a cheer, for within seconds the tree was shimmering with delicate pink blossom, so many thousands of blooms that the branches were hidden under a cloud of hanging flowers.

From the midst of all this blossom Sentaro-san's feet appeared, then his legs and finally the old man himself slid down the last few feet of trunk, still with his box. He bowed his head almost to the ground as the Shogun thanked him with a smile of pleasure. He himself gave the old man a cup of solid gold filled with the finest rice-wine, and when this was drunk rewarded him further with much gold and silver and other precious things. The Shogun ordered that henceforth the old man should be called *Hana-Saka-Jijii*, or 'The Old Man who makes the Trees Blossom'. All were to recognise him by that name and to afford him great honour.

So Sentaro-san returned home to his wife loaded with honours and the two of them spent many happy years in their little house surrounded by their beautiful garden, now very much enlarged by the purchase of their wicked neighbours' house and grounds. For the old couple deliberately paid them almost twice what it was worth—just to get rid of them!

Momotaro—The Peach Warrior

In a small wooden cottage near a lake at the foot of Mount Fuji there lived an old man and his wife. His name was Ojii-san and although he and his wife worked hard they were very poor. The husband went every day to the hills to cut grass, long tall Japanese grass, which he sold to the farmers for feeding their cattle. This was the only means he had of earning a living, such as it was, but they had a small rice field of their own which his wife O-Shino-san kept weeded and cultivated between sessions devoted to housework and preparing her husband's meals.

On this particular day Ojii-san had gone off as usual to the hills to cut grass while his wife piled clothes into a basket which she took down to the river to wash. It was a Good Luck Day in late spring and despite their poverty and their sadness at not having any children both husband and wife felt an extraordinary happiness so that O-Shino-san sang as she scrubbed and Ojii-san whistled as he worked.

The old woman had found a pleasant spot on the river bank beneath a group of pussy-willow trees. The water was crystal clear and she was about halfway through her task when something caused her to look up. Out of the corner of her eyes she had spotted something floating down towards her and to her amazement it turned out to be a very large peach.

'What a huge peach! And what a treat for my husband!'

The massive peach was floating out of her reach so she started to look around for a stick long enough to steer it to the bank. But there was no stick near that could reach the peach and she knew if she went off to find one it would have drifted down river and out of sight.

Suddenly, she remembered from her girlhood a charm-verse, as her mother called it, that was used by her father to bring fish within reach. Excitedly she began to clap her hands and sang:

> 'Distant water is bitter,
> The nearer water is sweet;
> Leave the distant water
> And come into the sweet.'

Strange to say, she had only sung the verse three times when the floating peach was seen to change direction, lapping nearer and nearer the bank where O-Shino-san was standing. Finally it stopped just in front of her and she was able to reach down and pick it from the water.

She was so delighted that she abandoned any further attempt at clothes washing and picked up the basket and hurried home with her prize. She placed the heavy peach carefully on a table and sat down on the tatami floor to await the return of her husband. The hours went by as she waited impatiently, but at last, just as the sun was setting, she made out Ojii-san's figure through the trees, the bundle of grass on his back so large it hid all but his legs and feet.

'Ojii-san! I've been waiting hours for you! You'll never guess what I've found!'

'Found, wife? What have you found?'

'Look! Here on the table! It's a present for you!'

Ojii-san was washing his feet in the basin of water his wife had placed near the entrance. Then, after drying them, he stepped on to the verandah and into the room. When he saw the peach he could

hardly believe his eyes and gasped with astonishment.

'Where on earth did you buy this? It's the largest peach I've ever seen, or am ever likely to see!'

'I didn't buy it, husband. I found it floating in the river.'

'Wherever you got it, let's sample it now, for I've not eaten a bite since midday.'

His wife was smiling and nodding her head as she hurried to get the kitchen knife. Her husband took the knife and was about to cut the peach in two when, wonderful to tell, the peach suddenly split in equal halves and a clear voice said: 'Wait a bit, old man!'

And out of the space in the centre of the fruit stepped a beautiful little child.

Ojii-san and his wife were so astonished and fearful that they threw themselves prostrate on the tatami floor with their heads pressed hard to the ground.

'Good people, don't be afraid. I am no demon. The gods have had compassion on you for every night you have both lamented that you had no child. Your cry has been heard and I am sent to be the son of your old age!'

At this the old man and his wife were so joyful that they could only rise to their knees and embrace. The little boy stood there smiling at their delighted faces. Taking courage Ojii-san tenderly picked up the child. Then O-Shino-san did the same, tears of gratitude streaming down her face.

Later, after he had eaten the food they gave him, they made the boy a bed in a drawer and tucked him up to sleep. The old couple sat far into the night discussing their good luck and the plans they had for the future of their little son. They named him Momotaro, which means Son of a Peach, for that was where he had come from.

The years passed happily now that the old people had a fine young son and the lad grew to normal size in less than a year and, by the time he was fifteen years of age, such was their care of him, that he was taller and far stronger than any other boy of his years. He had a handsome face and a heart full of courage, was kind and considerate to his parents, and clever in all his ways. The old couple's pleasure was very great and they thought the young man was just what a hero ought to be like. They loved him very dearly.

Then came the day when he told them that he must away and seek his fortune in order to repay in some measure their kindness over many years. In vain the old couple protested that they had done no more than their duty to a good son, just as other parents would, and that he owed them nothing—nothing at all!

'I hope you will be patient with me,' said Momotaro, 'and I know you think it strange that I wish to go away. But I promise to come back.'

'But where are you going?'

Momotaro hesitated. 'I fear you will be alarmed about my safety, but I have magical powers not given to many men. Don't be anxious when I tell you that I am off to Demons' Island.'

'Demons' Island!'

'There is an island in the sea to the north-east of Japan that is a

80

stronghold for a band of devils.'

'We know! We know! But no man can defeat them!'

Momotaro smiled. 'I came from the gods and the gods will protect me. Fear not, Father and Mother, for I promise to be back before the next full moon.'

Much more was said before he partly allayed their fears but once they realised how determined the lad was the old couple consulted together and finally gave their consent to the journey. O-Shino-san at once set to work to pound rice in the kitchen mortar to make cakes to sustain him, while Ojii-san gave him a packet of dried squid and a flask of *sake*.

Soon after dawn next day Momotaro bade them goodbye, bowed low in respect, then stepped quickly out of the house to be lost to sight amidst the trees. He travelled fast until midday when, feeling hungry, he sat down under the shade of a tall tree and opened the bag of rice cakes. As he began to eat the first one a large dog came runing up. It was dressed in a red kimono and had samurai swords in its belt, so Momotaro was not in the least surprised to hear it address him and beg one of his rice cakes.

'Know you, my fine dog, that I am Momotaro and I am off to the Isle of Demons to fight and defeat them and capture their treasure. You must earn your rice cake by promising to come with me as one of my samurai.'

The dog bowed low and immediately agreed, so Momotaro gave him a rice cake and off they set on their journey.

For several hours they walked through woods, hills, and valleys, then suddenly a monkey, dressed in a bright blue kimono and with samurai swords in its belt, rose from the path before them and bowed low.

'Good afternoon, Momotaro! You are welcome to this part of the country. May I have one of your rice cakes?'

Momotaro answered him as he had the dog and the monkey as quickly agreed, was given his rice cake, and off they started once more.

By and by they came to a field carpeted with flowers, and they had just reached its centre when a large pheasant flew down. It was the most beautiful bird Momotaro had ever seen, for on its body were five different robes of feathers and its head was covered with a scarlet cap. Round its waist was a silken belt in which hung two samurai swords.

'Good day, Momotaro! Welcome to north-east Japan. May I have one of your rice cakes?'

Momotaro answered the pheasant just as he had the dog and the monkey and the pheasant just as quickly accepted the challenge. So our young warrior gave him a rice cake and off they started once more.

The land they were passing through had been devastated by repeated marauding attacks by the demons. Men, women, and children had been carried off on numerous occasions, never to be heard of again. But word had somehow gone before him that Momotaro-san was on his way to avenge these wicked raids and the villages they passed through were alive with waving paper flags and bunting and cries of 'Momotaro-san! Momotaro-san! Our hero! Our hero!'

The dog, the monkey and the pheasant strode purposefully forward, looking as grim as possible, and the young warrior who led them did not permit himself a single wave or bow. They were samurai, and in their presence the waiting crowds bowed low, many kneeling with their foreheads in the dust.

That night they camped on the shore of the North-East Sea near the

mouth of a river where, by what means they could not tell, a ship with furled sails lay anchored ready for their journey. By dawn they were all aboard and, as the wind blew in their favour, they cut through the waves towards the horizon until the sight of a distant island met the eyes of the four sworded warriors.

Momotaro called the pheasant to him.

'Fly at once to the castle you will find on the island, and engage the devils in a fight. While they are engaged with you we will sail directly to the shore and storm the castle from the ground.'

The big bird saluted and instantly obeyed, flying high over the sea to perch finally on the topmost tower of the castle. There he shouted down to the demons clustered below him, challenging them to fight.

'Listen to me, you devils! The great Japanese general Momotaro-san has come to take your castle from you. If you wish to save your lives surrender at once. In token of your submission you must each break off the horns you have on your foreheads! Do this at once or we will kill you all!'

The horned demons burst into laughter, then rushed to put on tiger-skin trousers in order to look even more terrible and instil fear in their foes. Each was armed with a long iron spear and the foremost of them started to climb up to where the pheasant perched, only to be instantly attacked by the bird. It circled behind the leading climbers, driving its sharp beak into the back of their heads with such force that several of them fell from the battlements and were badly injured.

Meanwhile, Momotaro and his two faithful samurai had landed, only to discover that the castle was surrounded by high walls and was strongly fortified. The shore was like a precipice, so he ran with the dog and the monkey along its length hoping to find some way of scaling the cliffs. Suddenly they came upon two beautiful girls who appeared to be washing blood-stained clothes in a stream, and as they washed tears were cascading down their cheeks.

'Who are you, and why do you weep?'

The girls looked startled until he reassured them, when they haltingly told him that they were captives of the Demon King.

'We were abducted from our homes on their last raid on the

mainland, and even though we are the daughters of rich and powerful lords our fathers have failed to rescue us.'

'But why wash clothes?'

'We can't help it! We are obliged to be his servants, though we know that one day he will surely kill and eat us'—here one of them held up the blood-stained clothes—'just as he did the poor unfortunate creature these once belonged to!'

'Your days of trouble are over,' said Momotaro, 'only dry your tears for we are going to rescue you and all the other prisoners.'

'Bless you, sir, and your brave companions.'

'Show us the way into the castle for there is not a moment to be lost!'

The sounds of screams and of clashing metal could be heard coming from behind the fortress's walls as the pheasant battled against increasing odds, hoping desperately that his three friends would soon appear. Momotaro followed quickly behind the girls as they ran up the beach to where a secret door was let into the bottom of

the cliff. As soon as they pointed to it our three warriors were through it and racing up the steep flight of stone stairs that led to the castle.

Just in time they burst into the courtyard, now not only covered with dead and injured demons but with handfuls of feathers plucked from the brave bird still fighting above them. Momotaro's onslaught was so furious that his first sword stroke severed not one but three of the demons' heads, while his two companions wreaked havoc at the other side of the yard.

It soon became obvious that the fight was becoming one-sided. Momotaro and his three samurai were but four in all, but they fought like a hundred warriors, or so it seemed to the demons. They were now in full retreat, some trying desperately to break off their horns to surrender, but they were driven on to the parapet of the castle in a screaming mob, dozens falling over the battlements to be dashed to pieces on the rocks below; others fell into the sea and were drowned; while our four heroes made short work of the rest.

At last only the Chief Devil was left, having kept well out of the fighting as soon as he saw which way the battle was going. He had made up his mind to surrender before the four warriors made their final charge with swords held above their heads so that the last of the minor devils fell to his death. The demon approached humbly, both hands held high in the air, throwing down his iron spear as he did so. Kneeling at Momotaro's feet he broke off first one horn from his forehead and then the second, in token of complete submission. They were the evil signs of the devils' magical powers. Without their two curved horns their strength soon ebbed and then drained away forever.

'Great General,' said the demon meekly, 'I submit to your mercy. All my band are scattered or dead and I cannot stand against you.'

Momotaro laughed.

'Mercy! For you!'

'Great Master, I will give you all the treasure hidden in this castle if only you will spare my life.' He put his hand to his head to feel if the stumps of his horns were bleeding. 'I am powerless, so please have mercy!'

Once again Momotaro laughed.

'Fancy the Chief of the Devils begging for mercy! But I have not the least intention of sparing your wicked life however much you may beg. You have killed and tortured and eaten many innocent people and terrorised the lands about here for many years. Now you must suffer your fate!'

Suddenly the demon twisted himself free, attempting to pick up his broken horns from the monkey's feet who promptly kicked them away. And then, seeing all was lost, the demon ran to the battlements pursued by the dog and the pheasant, who almost caught him just as he jumped far out to hit the waves below with a resounding splash! He bobbed to the surface for an instant and then sank beneath the waters of the sea.

Momotaro and his followers now went through all the rooms of the castle, setting prisoners free and gathering up all the treasure. Chest after chest was crammed with gold and precious stones, silver and jewellery of every kind, ropes of pearls and dishes of pure gold, so that they had to recruit help from some of the prisoners they had so recently set free in order to carry home their plunder.

The two beautiful girls, daughters of lords, and others whom the wicked demon had carried off to be his slaves, were delivered safely back into the arms of their parents and friends amongst much rejoicing.

The whole country made a hero of Momotaro on his triumphant return, and he and his three warriors were treated almost as gods. Festivities lasted many days, for there was no more fear of the demons and the terror was banished from the land.

Finally, Momotaro-san arrived back at the home of his old parents, and great was their joy and pride in the one they still thought of as their little Son of the Peach. The treasure their boy had brought home with him enabled them all to live in peace and tranquillity to the end of their days.

The Matsuyama Mirror

Long years ago in a very remote province of Old Japan there lived a man and his wife whose life had been made very happy by the birth of a little daughter. They both loved her with all their hearts and marked all the customary ceremonies in her honour. She was carried to the temple when just thirty days old, her proud mother wearing a ceremonial kimono for the child had to be put under the patronage of the family's household god. Later there was the daughter's first dolls' festival when her parents gave her sets of dolls and their miniature belongings, the collection to be added to with each succeeding year. They had named her Sachiko, which in English means 'Happy Child', and so she proved to be. Then came a most important occasion, for on her third birthday Sachiko was given her first *obi*, a broad brocade sash of pure silk in colours of scarlet and gold. It was tied round her slim little waist and very pretty she looked in it. It was a sign that she had now left infancy behind and had crossed the threshold into girlhood.

One day, when Sachiko was seven years of age, there was much excitement in the home for her father had been suddenly summoned to the capital. He would be away for several weeks for Kyoto was many hundreds of miles from Matsuyama, the roads in parts being almost non-existent, so he would have to walk most of the way.

'Do not be anxious, wife. I will be back by the second full moon. Take care of everything, and especially of our little daughter.'

As the father turned from a distance to take a last look at his weeping wife and his smiling eager child he felt as if someone was pulling him back by his hair, so hard was it to leave a family from which he had never before been parted.

The weeks went by and Sachiko did her best to help her mother in the house and garden for she had promised her father to be a good girl.

'When father comes home again, how happy I shall be!' she said to her mother every week. 'It won't be long now, Mummy.'

At last the time came when her father was expected back and all was hurry and bustle in their wooden home. The mother dressed herself in her blue kimono, the colour her husband liked best, and her little daughter was bathed and brushed and combed and went to meet her father wearing her fine silk dress with its design of chrysanthemums.

Anyone who did not know him well would have had difficulty in recognising her father. He had travelled day after day exposed to all weathers and was sunburned to bronze. But his loving wife and daughter knew him at a glance and ran to meet him, each catching hold of one of his wide silk sleeves in the eagerness of their greeting.

Soon they were in the house and sitting cross-legged on the warm tatami floor, and no sooner had her father been refreshed with the food and drink his wife had set before him than he beckoned to Sachiko to come nearer and bring him the bamboo basket he had taken on his travels. His daughter watched with rapidly beating heart as he pulled the strings and took off the woven lid, leaning forward as her father put his hand inside.

'Here is a present for a good girl,' and her father smiled as he handed his daughter a beautifully-made doll and a lacquer box full of little cakes. 'It is a prize for taking care of your mother and the house and garden so well while I was away.'

'Thank you,' said the child, bowing her head to the ground, then putting out her hand with eager outstretched fingers to take the doll and the box. Coming from Kyoto, the then capital of Japan, both box and doll were finely made and prettier, she thought, than anything she had ever seen. She was delighted with her presents and hugged them to her, not touching the cakes for days so as not to spoil the anticipation of their eating.

Again the husband put his hand in the basket, this time bringing out a square wooden box tied up with red and white string.

'And this is for you,' he said with a slight bow as he handed it over to his wife.

Trying not to appear too eager, she took it from him, opening it carefully as Sachiko watched her with wondering eyes. From out of the box she took what appeared to be a metal disc with a handle attached. One side was bright and shining like crystal, while the other was covered with raised figures of pine-trees and storks carved out of its surface in lifelike reality. Never had she seen anything like it, for she had been born and bred in rural Matsuyama far from any town. She gazed into the shining metal disc then started in surprise so that she almost dropped it.

'Husband! Husband! I see someone looking at me in this round thing! Honourable husband, what is it you have given me?'

Her husband laughed. 'It is your own face that you see. What I have brought you is called a mirror and whoever looks into its clear surface sees their own form reflected there. This may be the only one in the whole of Echigo province, but in the capital they have been used since ancient times.'

He laughed again at her puzzled face, taking it from her so that he was himself reflected in its surface.

'There is an old proverb which says: "As the sword is the soul of a samurai, so is the mirror the soul of a woman". Tradition has it that a woman's mirror is a token of her character—if she keeps it bright and clear so is her heart pure and good. It is also one of the treasures which form the insignia of the Emperor, so you must lay great store by your mirror and use it carefully.'

His wife listened to all her husband told her, and was more than pleased at the precious gift—his token of remembrance while he had been away.

She bowed low again to her husband, then again gazed into the metal disc.

'Husband, I see a pretty woman looking at me and moving her lips as though she was speaking, and, strangest of all, she has on a blue kimono very much like mine.'

He laughed again, telling her to listen once more as he explained the mirror's qualities for she had plainly not understood.

'Silly woman, it is your own face that you see.'

The wife was as charmed with her present as little Sachiko with hers. For the first few days the mother could not look in the mirror often enough, but she came to consider that such a wonderful thing was too precious for everyday use. She laid it in its box again and put it away carefully amongst her most valued treasures.

Time passed away in their peaceful home and the parents saw their fondest hopes realised as their daughter grew from childhood into a beautiful girl of sixteen. She had grown up to be the very image of her mother and was so dutiful and affectionate that everyone loved her.

The mother kept the mirror hidden carefully away, mindful of her own passing vanity at discovering her own beauty when first looking into it. Seeing her own face might make Sachiko equally vain. So it happened that the daughter grew up as innocent of her beauty as her mother had been, or of the mirror which would have reflected her prettiness.

Then came the awful day when the mother was suddenly taken ill; although her daughter waited upon her night and day with all her loving care she gradually sank lower and lower as the illness ran its course. The village doctor could do no more and sorrowfully shook his head, until finally, knowing she had only days to live, the mother called her daughter to her.

'My darling child, you know that I must soon leave you. When I am gone promise me that you will look into this mirror every night and every morning. There you will see me and know that I am watching over you.'

With these words the mother took the mirror from its hiding place beneath the mattress she was lying on and gave it to her daughter. The young girl promised, with many tears, to do as her mother wished, whereupon the dying woman smiled and reached out and held Sachiko's hand. She passed into a deep and tranquil sleep from which she did not return.

The girl never forgot her mother's last request and every morning and evening she took the mirror from its box and looked into it long and earnestly. There she saw the bright and smiling face of her lost mother, not pale and sickly as in her final days, but the beautiful young mother of long ago. Every night Sachiko told her the story of the day's trials and tribulations, and in the morning she looked to her mother for sympathy and encouragement in whatever the day might have in store.

The weight of sorrow gradually lifted from her young heart and daily she grew in the likeness of her mother's character. She was gentle and kind to all and a helpful and dutiful daughter to her father, and even when he married again she did her best to like her new stepmother. However, this proved to be no easy task for her father's new wife was not only petty and mean over little things, but jealous of her husband's love of his pretty daughter. There had been rumours in the village that she practised spells and that she had managed to bewitch Sachiko's father into marrying her. This saddened Sachiko even further for she feared her stepmother would charm away the love her father always lavished on her, so she now consulted her mother's image each morning and evening for longer periods.

It was her step-daughter's absence in her room that aroused the spellbinder's suspicions so that she became determined to find out who or what it was the girl was talking to. Several times she had heard Sachiko's whispered tones through the sliding paper door, but each time she had tried to open it a crack she had found the latch bolted. That brat was up to something, that was sure!

After a further week of frustration she could stand it no more, so despite the risk of discovery she hurried out to a secret cave in the woods where she kept her spells and charms and within minutes had changed herself into a sharp-toothed rat. Anyone walking there might have seen the rodent scurrying back to Sachiko's house, then across the garden and in through a partly open door. The stepmother knew that the girl kept a ventilation panel between her room and the next open in the summer and it was to this she scurried, quietly clawing her way up the paper-panels to reach it. The rat cautiously put its head through the gap. Sachiko was kneeling with her back towards the panel, so the rat, not knowing it was a mirror that the girl held in her hands, slowly crept down the wall to hear what she was saying.

'Mother, I have been today what you would have me be, but my heart is heavy. I fear my father loves me less and less, and although I do my best to please my stepmother I feel she resents my presence and wishes me away. Dear Mother, what shall I do?'

Sachiko watched her own lips moving and asking the question in the silver mirror, then, as she remained silent, the face in the mirror suddenly spoke of its own accord.

'My dear Sachiko, I am here to guard over you. Turn down this present your father once brought home to me. Turn its face so that you can see the floor behind you. Daughter of mine, do as I tell you!'

The last words were a command so strictly said that the girl instinctively obeyed, changing the angle of the mirror so that the floor behind her came into view. There sat a large grey rat, its paw cupped to its ear the better to hear what passed. Instantly the girl screamed in horror, and then gave another loud-pitched cry for help as the rat turned to flee. But the girl reached the door first, snatching back the bolt and flinging it open as her father rushed into the room.

'A rat! A rat! Oh Father, help me!'

Now the rat had reached halfway up the panels towards the gap the ventilator left open, but Sachiko's father knocked it aside with his sword, slashing it in half at a stroke as it struggled to rise to its feet.

As he did so it was as though a great weight was lifted from the shoulders of father and daughter, and he turned and tenderly put his arms around the white-faced girl.

The rat's body he cast into the river, and neither of them ever mentioned the stepmother's name again or asked where she had gone to. She was seen no more and both father and daughter lived happily as the years passed by. Long, long after the events you have just read, the day came when Sachiko handed over the mirror to her own little daughter and watched over her and guarded her just as her own mother had done. And she in her turn lived happily ever after.

The Wooden Bowl

Once upon a time there lived an old Japanese couple who had seen far better days. Formerly, when they were young and strong, they had been quite well-to-do, but misfortune came upon them when they least expected it to and now, in their old age, they had become so poor that it was all they could do to earn their daily bread.

One joy, however, remained to them. They had been blessed with a beautiful young daughter, kind-hearted and hard-working and so modest that to glance in a mirror caused her to blush at her own prettiness. When her father fell sick she and her mother worked day and night to nurse him back to health, but he got out of bed too soon, had a relapse and suddenly died. Great was their sorrow!

Now the mother and daughter had to work harder than ever to earn their daily bread, but just as they thought they were a little better off the mother felt her strength was failing. She said nothing to her daughter Ochiyo-san, and the girl worked on in ignorance of her mother's rapidly deteriorating condition until one day she discovered the old lady collapsed on the floor.

By this time Ochiyo-san's beauty had become so dazzling that it was the cause of much heart-searching by the dying mother. She knew

97

only too well that in one so poor and friendless as her daughter such beauty was more likely to be a misfortune rather than a blessing. So each time Ochiyo-san was away tending their small field of rice the old lady prayed long and earnestly to her gods, beseeching them to help her save her daughter from any harm. The days passed into weeks but still she prayed, each day growing weaker and weaker, when suddenly, one warm and sunny afternoon, she experienced a sense of relief and at the same time felt that some object had appeared on her bed of sickness. Raising her head to look down towards her feet Ochiyo's mother perceived a large bowl of lacquered wood placed upside-down on the bedclothes. Why upside-down? Then a voice inside her head spoke with the tongue of the god and the old lady relaxed back on her pillow smiling gratefully.

Next morning, feeling her end to be very near, she called her daughter to her and with many words of love entreated her to be pure and good and true as she had always been.

'Your beauty is a perilous gift, Ochiyo, which may well become your ruin. Please do not question why I ask you to wear this, but only believe your mother when I tell you it is the work of the gods.'

The old lady's strength was nearly gone, but reaching for the lacquered bowl by one final effort she managed to place it on her daughter's head. The bowl completely overshadowed the girl's face so it was impossible to tell whether beauty was hidden beneath it or not. Witnessing what she had done the old woman smiled contentedly then lay back and closed her eyes.

Now that her mother was gone Ochiyo-san was indeed forlorn, but she had a brave heart and at once set about earning her living by hard work in the fields. She was never seen without the wooden bowl, a head-dress which much amused the village people, and it was not long before she was known to everyone as the Maid with the Bowl on her Head. Some of the idle young men of the village made fun of her and tried to peep under the bowl and even to pull if off her head. But it was firmly fixed and not one of them ever succeeded in getting so much as a glimpse of the whole of her face so that word got around that she wore it to hide her ugliness. In the end they tired of teasing her

and left her alone to her own devices.

One day, when she was at work helping a rich farmer to harvest his crop, the owner himself drew near to watch her. He was immediately struck by Ochiyo-san's gentle and modest behaviour and by her quickness and diligence at her work, so much so that he kept her employed right to the end of the harvest. After that, with winter soon coming on, he gave her a place in his own house to wait upon his wife who had long been sick and seldom left her bed. So the poor orphan girl had a happy home once more, for both the farmer and his wife were very kind to her. As they had no daughter of their own she soon became more like a child of the house rather than a hired servant. Indeed, no child could have made a gentler or more tender nurse to the sick wife than did Ochiyo-san to her mistress.

After some months, there was great excitement for the master's eldest son was to return home from the capital, Kyoto. In this rich and sophisticated city he had learned much, but had at last become wearied by too much feasting and pleasure and was more than glad to come back to the quiet country home of his childhood. Week after week passed, but to the surprise of his city friends Masanori-san stayed on in the country, appearing quite content with the rural life and showing no desire to go back to the stir and excitement of the town.

The truth was, however, that he had accidentally caught a glimpse of the face of the Maid with the Bowl on her Head. Ochiyo-san was kneeling feeding the golden carp in the sunlit pool in the garden when Masanori-san came up to stand behind her. Looking down he could see most of her face reflected on the clear surface of the water and instantly decided that this gentle and beautiful girl should one day become his wife.

When the news filtered through the family of the eldest son's desire there were many amongst the older female relatives who were completely scandalised. Two of his old maiden aunts were especially bitter in their comments.

'She may well be a hard worker, but she's only a servant! And why on earth does the master permit her to go around with that ridiculous bowl on her head? If you ask me it's to hide her ugliness!'

Even her sick old mistress seemed to turn against her and she had no friend in the house except her master. He would have been pleased to welcome Ochiyo-san as his daughter-in-law but did not dare say as much.

Despite all this opposition, to everyone's surprise Masanori-san remained quite determined to marry the girl. As to all the stories his old aunts and others brought him he made it quite clear he considered them no more than a pack of ill-natured lies.

After many months, seeing the young man so steadfast in his determination and perceiving that their opposition made him even more obstinate, they were forced to give in, but with a bad grace.

However, to their utter surprise, the poor little Maid with the Bowl on her Head upset all their calculations by gratefully but firmly refusing the hand of the master's eldest son, and no persuasion on his part could make her change her mind. Great was the astonishment and anger of the son's relations. That they should be made fools of in this way was beyond all bearing. Did she think the master's son was not good enough for her?

Had they but known it, Ochiyo-san's heart was close to breaking. She loved Masanori-san greatly but she could not bear to bring strife and discord into a family home which had sheltered her from poverty. She had marked the cold looks of the aunts and her mistress and well knew what they meant. Rather than bring trouble she would leave the house for ever. She shed many bitter tears, but told no one of her intention of leaving first thing in the morning.

That night the poor girl cried herself to sleep, a deep slumber in which her mother suddenly appeared before her. While in her dream Ochiyo-san bowed low before the old lady, she was told that the gods had decreed that she might, without scruple, marry the man whom she loved. She awoke full of joy and when the young man once more entreated her to marry she answered, 'Yes! Yes! Yes!' with all her heart.

'We told you so!' said the mother and the aunts, but young Masanori-san was far too happy to mind them.

So the wedding day was fixed amidst the grandest preparations for a magnificent feast. Some unpleasant remarks could still be heard about a beggar maid marrying a young noble, but the young man took absolutely no notice. On the great day all the company assembled ready to assist in the ceremony, and it seemed to everyone, not least the bride-to-be herself, that the time had come to remove the large black lacquered bowl she had worn so long on her head. She tried to take it off, but found to her dismay that she could not move it. Then the guests joined in, but when they tried to pull off the bowl it uttered loud cries and groans as of pain. This so startled them that they backed away in fright.

The bridegroom comforted and consoled Ochiyo-san for she was now close to tears. He insisted that the ceremony should go ahead, wooden bowl or no wooden bowl. The priests did their part until the moment when the rice-wine cups were brought in. The bride and groom must drink together the wedding cup, three times three, in token that they were now man and wife.

As the bride raised the cup to her lips for the third time a loud cracking noise was heard and as she sipped the *sake* the wooden bowl on her head suddenly broke into dozens of pieces, falling to the floor amidst a shower of diamonds, rubies, emeralds, pearls, and other precious stones, together with pieces of gold and silver in abundance. It was her marriage portion, her dowry from the gods, and a cry of joy went up throughout the room.

But what astonished the wedding guests even more than all this treasure was the wonderful beauty of the bride. For the first time they could see and appreciate the beauty of her face. Her husband, who had previously caught only a glimpse in the water of the pool, was overjoyed that he had kept faith with the Maid with the Bowl on her Head.

Needless to say, they all lived happily ever after!

The Ogre of Rashomon

Long ago in Kyoto, the capital of Old Japan, the people of the city used to cower in fear each night, trembling in their flimsy wood and paper houses at the dreadful cries they could hear coming from the direction of the Rashomon Gate.

It was known that, as soon as darkness fell, a dreadful ogre left his cave in the hills to lurk at this particular gate of the city, waiting to seize any human unfortunate enough to pass near. The men, women and children he grabbed were never seen again and it was whispered that the horrible creature was a cannibal who made a meal of his victims long before the sun rose over the eastern hills. Because no one had ventured near the gate for many nights the ogre was ravenous, and he had now taken to tearing down houses near the gate, plucking his screaming victims from out of cupboards, under staircases, from garden out-houses, or wherever else they might be hiding.

Now at that time there lived in a castle near Kyoto a famous general named Raiko, whose brave deeds included killing the chief of a band of ogres by cutting off his head at a single stroke despite the fact that the creature's neck was as thick as the trunk of a tree. And a very big tree, at that!

This brave warrior was always followed by a band of faithful knights. One evening these five knights sat at a feast to celebrate yet another victory, drinking *sake* in their rice bowls, and eating all kinds of raw fish which they picked up with their chopsticks, dipped in soy sauce, and then popped the slices and rice-balls wrapped in seaweed into their mouths. Every few minutes one or other of them would toast the health of his comrades-in-arms, the glasses clinking together to cries of '*Kanpai! Kanpai!* Good Health! Good Health!'

It was then that the knight Hojo turned to his companions to ask them if they had heard the rumours that every evening after sunset an ogre came to the Gate of Rashomon in Kyoto and that he seized and devoured all who passed by?

Watanabe, who sat crossed-legged next to him, answered by saying: 'This cannot be true, my friend. All the ogres were killed by our chief Raiko at Oeyama. Even if one escaped he would not dare show himself, knowing full well that we would attack him as we had done his master and that he would suffer the same fate!'

'Then you disbelieve what I say?'

'No, not in that sense, but you have probably heard some old woman's exaggerated story and taken it for true.'

Hojo's face reddened, but he controlled himself.

'Then perhaps, Watanabe-san, you might like to prove or disprove what I say by going yourself to the Rashomon Gate and lingering there for an hour or so!'

No samurai knight hesitates for a second where his honour and courage are at stake and Watanabe-san was no exception.

'Of course! The sun has long since set so I am off to seek Hojo's ogre!'

Watched by his four companions with amused interest Watanabe buckled on his two swords and put on his coat of armour. Finally he clamped his helmet on his head and made a bow as he prepared to leave.

'Give me something, so that I can prove I have been there!'

One of the knights produced a roll of writing paper and a box of Indian ink and brushes. First he signed himself, then passed the

brush to his three friends in turn. All signed their names before handing the paper to Watanabe-san.

'I will nail this to the Gate of Rashomon this very night. Tomorrow you can each of you go and look at it. Let us hope I catch not one ogre but half a dozen!'

There was neither moon nor stars to light Watanabe-san on his way, but his horse knew the road and within two hours he reached the dreaded gate.

'Just as I thought,' said Watanabe-san, 'not an ogre to be seen! An old woman's story, I'll be bound!'

He felt for the paper and had just pinned it to the gate when he became aware that he was not alone. For a second the hair stood upright on the back of his neck as he smelled the foetid breath that hallmarked every ogre in Japan. Next second a huge hand plucked at his helmet and attempted to get a grip around his throat.

Every samurai warrior prides himself on being able to draw his long sword and strike a man down in a single movement, but to be grasped by the neck from behind and instantly wound your attacker was no easy task. But every warrior had practised and practised such a movement and in a flash Watanabe-san had curved his sword in a back-sweeping arc that drew forth a deep-throated scream of pain from the huge creature intent on strangling him. Then Watanabe-san's eyes grew round in wonder as he saw for the first time the size of the enemy who faced him. The ogre was far taller than the great gate

105

itself, his eyes were flashing mirrors, and from his cavern-like mouth issued forth smoke and flames.

Watanabe-san never flinched and despite the flames he dashed in and attacked. The ogre seemed incapacitated in some way, but the darkness and the smoke made it very difficult to see how he had been wounded. Finally, in the face of Watanabe-san's incessant attacks, the huge monster turned and fled, at the same time vowing vengeance on the samurai who had defeated him.

Watanabe-san was close to exhaustion and sat panting on his horse before turning to leave for home. As he did so the horse shied and kicked to one side. There was something lying in the road and Watanabe-san gingerly dismounted and approached what seemed to be the trunk of a tree. A hairy tree at that, a tree which yielded as he kicked it so that his booted foot sank into it! Then suddenly he realised! It was the ogre's right arm! That first arcing blow must have severed it at a stroke!

Watanabe-san stooped to pick it up, groaning a little at the weight, but elated at having secured such a prize. This was the best of all proofs that he had really fought the ogre and vanquished him! He was a happy man as he rode home that night, the massive arm slung across the front of his saddle and lashed into place with the cord of his robe.

Late though it was he roused his sleeping companions and held aloft a lantern so that they could stare in wonderment at the hairy arm with its hand of talons which he had placed on the floor of the ante-room. All of them cheered and called him the hero of their band, and the next day was reserved for feasting at which Watanabe-san was the guest of honour. His wonderful deed was soon known throughout the city of Kyoto and people crowded in from near and far to see the ogre's awesome arm.

But within a day or two Watanabe-san began to grow anxious. He knew that the ogre he had wounded was still alive and might at any minute reappear to claim back his arm. How could it be kept safe and secure? He consulted his friends and together they sought out the best and most skilful carpenter in the whole of the city. Wanatabe-san ordered a box to be made of the strongest wood heavily banded with

iron and with the lid secured with a heavy chain and padlock. In this he placed the arm, locking the box and refusing to show the relic to anyone no matter how important they thought themselves. He kept the box in his own room and took charge of it himself, never letting it out of his sight.

One night, about a week later, he heard someone knocking at the porch and asking for admittance. When the servant went to the door to see who it was there was only an old woman, very respectable in her appearance. On being asked who she was and what was her business the old woman replied with a smile, saying that she had been a nurse to the master of the house when he was just a little baby. If the lord of the house was at home she begged to be allowed to see him.

The servant left the old woman at the door, closing it carefully behind her, and went to tell her master that his old nurse had come to see him. Watanabe-san thought it strange that she should come at that time of the night, but at the thought of the old woman who had tended and fed him as both a baby and a boy, and whom he had not seen for many years, he had not the heart to order her away. He told his servant to show her in.

In a few minutes the old woman was ushered into the room and she was indeed Watanabe-san's old nursemaid. Her face and figure had been imprinted on his mind and it was the same woman who now stood before him, bowing and greeting him with all the old fashioned courtesies.

'Master, the report of your brave fight with the ogre at the Gate of Rashomon is so widely known that even your poor old nurse has heard of it. Is it really true, what everyone says, that you cut off one of the ogre's arms? If you did, it is a deed to be highly praised!'

'It is true, old nurse, although I should have been better pleased if I could have killed the monster instead of only wounding him.'

'I am very proud to know that my little boy grew to manhood with so valiant a courage.' Here the old woman bowed very low. 'Before I die it is the great wish of my life to see the ogre's severed arm and I feel sure you will grant me this favour.'

Watanabe-san hesitated and turned to glance at the box in the corner of the room. Then he straightened himself and switched his gaze to the face of his old nurse.

'No,' he said. 'I am sorry, old lady, but I cannot grant your request.'

'But why?' asked the old woman, once again bowing low. 'It is such a small favour I ask.'

'Because,' replied Watanabe-san, 'ogres are very cunning and revengeful creatures. If I were to open the box there is no telling that he might suddenly appear in the hope of carrying off his arm. I have had the box specially made extremely strong and it is in there I keep the arm. I never show it to anyone, no matter what happens.'

'Your precaution is very reasonable,' smiled the old woman. 'But I am your old nurse who mothered you from birth to boyhood. Surely you will not refuse *me* the one favour I ask you?' She paused, but received no answer.

'Master, I have only just heard of your brave act, and not being able to wait until the morning I hurried round here immediately as fast as my old legs could carry me.'

Watanabe-san was very troubled by the old woman's pleading, but he still persisted in refusing. Then the old woman said: 'Surely, Master, you do not suspect me of being a spy sent by the ogre?'

It was Watanabe-san's turn to smile. 'Don't be foolish! I know my old nurse, and though your face and your figure and your voice are all older it is still my old *uba** who stands before me.'

'Then, Master, you will at least grant me my wish, the great wish of my heart, actually to see the arm of an ogre cut off by my brave hero!'

Watanabe-san could hold out no longer and beckoned her to the corner of the room where the large box with its chain and padlock stood.

'Now, stand back a little while I unlock the lid.'

The key grated and the chain fell to the floor. Watanabe-san took a deep breath and slowly lifted the heavy lid like that of a coffin, sliding it back against the wall.

'What is it like? Let me see! Let me see!'

As though fearful of actually seeing it the old woman edged herself slowly forward with little shuffling steps. She came nearer and nearer until she stood right against the box. Then suddenly, to Watanabe-san's astonished amazement, she plunged her left hand into the box, seized the arm, brandished it above her head, and cried out in a roaring voice that shook the room: 'My arm! My arm!'

Instantly, pandemonium reigned, the figure of the old nursemaid changing in seconds to the towering monster that was the ogre of Rashomon, and for once Watanabe-san was slow in drawing his sword. By the time he had done so the ceiling of the room had gone and so had the roof of the house as the ogre enlarged to his full size. With a roar he leapt high in the air and disappeared in a cloud of dust and smoke, leaving our brave warrior gnashing his teeth in rage and disappointment.

It was by this cunning trick that the ogre escaped with his arm, and though Watanabe-san haunted the Rashomon Gate for many a night the monster was never seen again. The people said the ogre was afraid of their great samurai warrior's strength and courage and had left the land forever.

So the citizens of Kyoto were able to go about their city even at night-time and Watanabe-san's brave deeds have never been forgotten, not even to the present day.

Uba = nursemaid